CLINICAL ASPECTS OF MALPRACTICE

CLINICAL ASPECTS OF MALPRACTICE

Robert S. Pollack, M.D.

Medical Economics Company Book Division
Oradell, New Jersey 07649

Design by Robert L. Pascoe
Cover design by JoAnne Cassella
Cover photo by Stephen E. Munz

ISBN 0-87489-230-9

Medical Economics Company
Oradell, New Jersey 07649

Printed in the United States of America

In memory of Edgar Allen Pollack, A.B., M.A., LL.B.
Father, teacher, counselor at law, he knew the true meaning of professional life.

Contents

Acknowledgments

Many sources contributed to this book. Thanks are due the physicians who gave their expertise, knowledge, and opinions; the hospitals that coded, translated, and provided their records; the numerous attorneys, both defendants' and plaintiffs', who offered their advice; the large malpractice insurance carriers for their cooperation and help; my secretary, Betty Brookes, for her expert typing and library research; and my wife, whose love, devotion, and encouragement made this book possible.

Robert S. Pollack, M.D.

Publisher's notes

Robert S. Pollack, M.D., is a diplomate of the American Board of Surgery and a past fellow of the American College of Surgeons. He is honorary and consulting surgeon at Presbyterian Hospital, San Francisco; attending surgeon at Children's Hospital and St. Francis Hospital, San Francisco; chief consulting surgeon, United States Public Health Service Hospital, San Francisco, and Veterans Administration hospitals, Martinez and Livermore; consulting surgeon, Travis Air Force Base Hospital; and clinical professor of surgery and oncology, University of the Pacific School of Dentistry, San Francisco. He was professor and director of the Department of General Surgery, University of California, Davis, and formerly maintained a private practice in general and cancer surgery in San Francisco.

Dr. Pollack is a graduate of Dartmouth College and Cornell University Medical College. His internship and residency were spent at The New York Hospital, the Hospital for Joint Diseases, and Memorial Sloan-Kettering Cancer Center, under the auspices of a National Cancer Institute fellowship. He is the author of three other books—*Tumor Surgery of the Head and Neck* (first edition, 1957; revised and expanded edition, 1975) and *Treatment of Breast Tumors* (1958)—and has contributed chapters to several surgical texts. He was an associate editor of *Oncology* and has published numerous articles in professional journals.

Throughout his distinguished career Dr. Pollack has taught, both in the United States and abroad. He has been a visiting professor and lecturer in many parts of the world. In the words of a colleague, he is "a surgeon's surgeon. Few contemporary surgeons enjoy his technical skill, ability, and experience. His scalpel is an artist's brush which he uses with reason and compassion."

Introduction

This book is written for physicians, by a physician, about the clinical problems of malpractice. It is based on an intensive review and analysis of hundreds of patients' charts and files in cases where malpractice action was threatened, initiated, settled, or tried in a court of law. As I studied each record, I looked for the medical or surgical cause of the complaint that led to malpractice action. Identifying these causes is one of the purposes of this book.

The other purpose is to emphasize what can be done to minimize the hazards of malpractice. Careful analysis of each case exposes specific pitfalls. Medical knowledge, clinical experience, and common sense suggest ways of avoiding these pitfalls.

There's no better way to enlighten the practicing physician than by clinical example. That's why the case reviews form the core of this book. They're arranged anatomically and presented from the physician's perspective in order to emphasize the responsibilities you assume in diagnosis and treatment.

The comments and discussions accompanying the case reviews pinpoint the mishap, the error in judgment, the laxity of office or clinic management, or the failure of technique that resulted in malpractice action. Some cases reveal a lack of knowledge on the part of patients or their families. Still others implicate greed or vindictiveness as the motive for litigation.

Because the emphasis of this book is clinical, not legal, cases were chosen to highlight the medical causes of malpractice action. The legal outcomes of the cases aren't always reported. Any suit, even though frivolous, costs the defendant money, time, reputation, and peace of mind. It's the fact that suit was threatened or brought, rather than the jury's decision or the amount of the settlement, that concerns us most.

The case reviews cover general problems commonly encountered by many physicians. Use of the terms *exposure* and *exposed* in the discussions is not meant to imply legal liability, nor should malpractice be inferred. These terms merely specify or illustrate the medical issues involved. Resemblance to individual cases currently under litigation is purely coincidental and inapplicable. All individuals are anonymous, and their identity should not be inferred from the content. Where necessary, details have been changed to prevent identification.

Surrounding the core of case reviews are more general discussions of the problems of malpractice and the physician's responsibility in obtaining informed consent, delegating work to subordinates, and hospitalizing patients. Finally, there's practical advice on how to conduct yourself as a defendant and as a witness in court cases.

Fortunately, only a small minority of patients regard any imperfection of treatment as grounds for a malpractice suit. The physician who fears every patient as a potential plaintiff is needlessly self-handicapped. Yet the legal risks of medical practice are real, and they have serious consequences for the doctor who disdains them. The golden mean between fear and overconfidence is to know where the risks lie and to take reasonable precautions against them.

Section I

Malpractice pitfalls

Medical Economics magazine seems to run a story on malpractice in almost every issue. These stories have two things in common: (1) The doctor in each case had provided competent care, and (2) he was astonished to be named as a defendant in a malpractice action. Unfortunately, not all these stories have a happy ending in common; if they did, there would be no reason to publish magazine stories, and no need for this book.

What can the conscientious physician do to minimize the risks of being sued for malpractice? The following six chapters examine the pitfalls inherent in the doctor-patient relationship and suggest steps you can take to strengthen your position in that relationship.

1

Patient rapport and informed consent

The ever-increasing sophistication of medical care that has developed simultaneously with an enlightened and critical laity has created an explosion of medical malpractice suits. Medical and surgical results at times fall short of expectations and objectives. Complications will occur. And, because doctors are only human, errors will be made.

The last three decades have produced a dramatic increase in the number, scope, and complexity of surgical operations, diagnostic techniques, and drugs. Ironically, these scientific advances have increased patients' vulnerability to the capriciousness of their own anatomy, physiology, and pathology—a fact few patients seem to accept. An atmosphere of distrust between the laity and the medical profession is symptomatic of the changing attitudes and expectations of today's society. The promise of expertise must be kept. Humanity has split the atom and walked on the moon. Nothing less than a comparable performance in health care can be considered acceptable. Failure is no longer tolerated.

Are patients—the consumers of health care—justified in this attitude? Whether they are or not, it's a fact of life. Doctors' vulnerability to charges of malpractice is well known. Arguing against the allegations in a suit is often difficult because of the very nature of human physiology and pathology. Gray zones surround human disease that defy the clear-cut guilty/not guilty answers the law demands. The success or failure of treatment can't fairly be attributed to human effort alone. Yet physicians often feel held accountable for what is beyond human comprehension.

Few lawyers clearly understand the true position of the doctor called upon to solve a medical problem. Whereas lawyers are used to working from known facts and precedents, to advocating a side in a dispute, and to accepting the decisions of juries and judges, doctors are trained to work from possible diagnoses, to be dispassionate, and to accept total responsibility for their actions. It's for this reason the chasm between lawyer and doctor yawns so wide; a chasm deepened by the feeling among many physicians that they're "sitting ducks" for any lawyer who decides to bring a suit, regardless of merit.

This attitude would explain and answer, if not fully, at least in part the charges and statements made by William J. Curran, J.D., L.M., S.M.Hyg., Professor of Legal Medicine, Harvard University, in his monograph *How Lawyers Handle Medical Malpractice Cases.*[1] In his study he exhibits surprise that doctors, as a whole, have such little sympathy and respect for the legal profession and captions one paragraph "The Hostility of Doctors Toward the Law." His words describe the collision course on which both professions are traveling:

> [The study] underscores one of the most important circumstances in this field: the huge cleavage between the legal profession in its beliefs and the medical profession and its beliefs. This is not merely a lack of interprofessional understanding, that common euphemistic cliché; it is evidence of outright hostility on the part of physicians toward the law and lawyers. The medical conceptions are all in one direction: Not one of them is favorable to the legal profession or to courts. They assume that unethical conduct and economic exploitation are widespread in the plaintiffs' bar. They assume that the law is unreasonable and prejudiced against doctors as a class.
>
> There is nothing new about hostility in the general public toward lawyers. Shakespeare and Dickens lead the way in English literature. "Ambulance chaser" has been an American term of derision in regard to personal injury plaintiffs' lawyers during all of this century. Physicians share some of these common prejudices. But there is more to it than this. The physicians' beliefs are very intense and firmly held.

That quotation is hard to argue against. But it must be pointed out that the beliefs and opinions of plaintiffs' attorneys are just as intense and as firmly held as those of physicians. What's often described as the "tunnel vision" of the physician toward malpractice applies equally to the "tunnel vision" of the attorney who will brook no other opinion than "guilty of malpractice" or "the facts speak for themselves." Fortunately, there exists a moderate middle ground.

Experienced clinicians know that the psychological factors of illness or disease breed an unconscious hostility toward themselves.[2] Patients tend to blame their doctors for the fear, sorrow, pain, and interruption of plans and ambitions they experience as a result of illness.[2] And the fact that patients are necessarily dependent on and subservient to the physician only adds to this unconscious hostility. Because many patients don't want to acknowledge this irrational attitude, even the most gentle, tactful, and kindly management will do little to change it. Fortunately, hostility is usually transient; as most patients recover, their attitude soon changes to appreciation and gratitude.

In those instances when unconscious hostility persists on the part of the patient or his relatives, it's often due to unavoidably disappointing results, complications, failure to heal, failure to cure, or continued pain. Hostility enhances the likelihood that the patient will sue the physician. The entire process then becomes a personal confrontation.

This is especially true of cancer patients. As Mittelmann and Scholhamer[2] recently stated, because of the potentially lethal nature of cancer, the thought processes of all persons connected with a case tend to be emotionally charged. Bigwood[3] noted Kübler-Ross's five stages through which many cancer patients pass: denial, anger, bargaining, depression, and acceptance.

To prevent or at least to minimize hostility and disappointment, you must establish rapport with the patient and obtain informed consent. If the planned surgical procedure or program of medical treatment carries a substantial risk of failure, tell the patient about it. Describe any alternative measures. Be sure he/she understands that doctors can't be certain whether one form of treatment or another is going to be successful in any individual patient. But tell him, too, that you prefer this particular procedure over any other because in your judgment it has the best chance of success. Note on the patient's chart the various procedures you've mentioned and the risks you've described.

In discussing the degree of risk, keep away from percentage figures or expressions, such as "the odds are two to one in your favor." Medicolegal experts cite several malpractice suits based on doctors' explanations in which percentages were used but later proved incorrect. The plaintiffs claimed that if the true percentages had been quoted, they wouldn't have agreed to the procedure. Stay with the medical facts and avoid statistics. Even though they may be accurate, the patient all too frequently will misinterpret their significance.

If you have good rapport with a patient and your explanation is geared to his understanding, he'll almost always consent to a procedure you are convinced is proper and necessary. However, suppose he won't listen to reason and remains recalcitrant. For example, you may be called to a patient's home or see him in the hospital emergency room. He is suffering from something as serious as acute appendicitis, a bleeding peptic ulcer, or severe congestive heart failure. Yet when you tell him he needs to be hospitalized for treatment, he refuses. "Treat me at home," he pleads. "Then, if I don't get better, I'll go into the hospital."

It's a difficult problem because you cannot admit him to the hospital against his will. If you give in to his request and attempt to treat him at home, you could be exposing him to serious, even fatal, consequences. In addition, you expose yourself to a potential malpractice charge.

"In such a case," says one medicolegal expert,[4] "the physician should take extraordinary steps to persuade the patient, even shock him into agreeing to be hospitalized. He should try to gain the patient's confidence to the extent that the patient will agree, however reluctantly, to being admitted. Failure to try is an indictment of the doctor's persuasive ability and might be construed by others as an attitude of indifference toward the patient. A demonstrated lack of interest makes the doctor legally culpable."

Suing for malpractice is almost wholly an American institution, perhaps partly because our legal system makes the courts available to all.[5] But other countries guarantee this right also. At the root of the growth of malpractice litigation are the high American standard of living, the American's expectation of perfection, his insistence on the best available, his tendency to question, and the fact that his high standard of living has made him "soft" about accepting serious disease and its consequences.

The American is a difficult patient to manage, compared with patients in other parts of the world. The paradox is that, despite its shortcomings, American medicine is very likely the best available anywhere.[6] Our teaching programs alone attest to this statement; thousands of non-American doctors enjoy our hospitality and then return to their homelands with enviable expertise.

References

1. Curran WJ: *How Lawyers Handle Medical Malpractice Cases: An Analysis of an Important Medicolegal Study*. Washington, DC: U.S. Department of Health, Education, and Welfare, Public Health

Service, Health Resources Administration, National Center for Health Services Research, DHEW publication No. (HRA) 76-3152
2. Mittelmann M, Scholhamer CF: Cancer and malpractice claims. *Cancer* 39:2573, 1977
3. Bigwood GF: Emotional reactions to cancer. *Lahey Clin Found Bull* 25:24, 1976
4. Hassard H: *Medical Malpractice: Risks, Protection, Prevention*. Oradell, NJ: Medical Economics Book Division, 1966
5. *Medical Malpractice: Report of the Secretary's Commission on Medical Malpractice*. Washington, DC: U.S. Department of Health, Education, and Welfare, DHEW publication No. (OS) 73-80:1-21, 1973
6. Welch CE: Medical malpractice. *N Engl J Med* 292:1372, 1975

2

Failure to diagnose; getting an autopsy

A dilemma confronting many conscientious physicians is presented by the patient afflicted with a disease that defies diagnosis. Failure to diagnose is a significant malpractice pitfall. It seems that patients expect nothing less than prompt, accurate diagnoses, no matter how silent or puzzling their signs and symptoms.

Many organizations that raise funds for medical research have public education programs calling attention to the dangers of a particular disease and its incidence, prevention, and treatment. The excellent work of these organizations is well known. But while they have undoubtedly contributed to improved diagnosis, treatment, and research, these public education programs have created a vexing paradox for physicians, as the following example shows.

Early detection of cancer has been a long-standing educational objective of the American Cancer Society. Its seven warning signals are universally displayed, and the public is constantly being reminded that when it's detected early, cancer can often be cured. But in its altruistic zeal, the society has unwittingly placed the dedicated physician in a predicament.

Given the idea that early detection of cancer means cure, the laity draws the simplistic conclusion that failure to cure results from late detection. When failure to cure is attributed to late diagnosis, despite the fact that early diagnosis may have been impossible, the implication is that the physician was negligent or incompetent. Hence the current spate of lawsuits alleging failure to diagnose cancer.

Emphasis on the early diagnosis of cancer ignores our scientific knowledge of the behavior of this disease. It's recognized that cure is more often a matter of the biologic function of the cell and the tumor-host relationship than of early diagnosis (see Chapter 46). But thanks to the emphasis on early detection, the public firmly equates failure to cure with failure to diagnose. The conscientious physician, who does his utmost to diagnose cancer as early as he can, finds himself defenseless.

The case studies that follow reveal that delay in diagnosis was attributed to various alleged omissions. In each case the plaintiff contended that had such failures not occurred, results would have been different. The most common omissions are (in no particular order, as each case presents individual malpractice problems):

1. Failure to take a complete history, especially drug sensitivity
2. Failure to keep accurate records
3. Failure to communicate with previous physicians who saw the patient
4. Failure to perform a complete physical examination, especially:
    - Oral cavity
    - Breasts
    - Pelvic area
    - Rectum
5. Failure to examine breasts and do pelvic examination on patients receiving hormones over a prolonged period
6. Failure to take Papanicolaou smears of cervix and vagina
7. Failure to perform or refer for biopsy
8. Failure to utilize appropriate laboratory tests
9. Failure to take X-rays of chest with posteroanterior and lateral projections; mammograms; gastrointestinal studies
10. Failure to recommend consultation
11. Failure to perform follow-up examinations and schedule prompt revisits in office or hospital.

Not included above are errors in interpretation of microscopic slides by pathologists or of X-ray films by roentgenologists. When malignant melanomas are called benign junctional nevi, infiltrating duct breast cancers called sclerosing adenosis, or malignant lymphomas called hyperplastic nodes, responsibility for failure to diagnose is readily apparent. The reverse situation, as when hyperplastic nodes are called a malignant lymphoma, has also resulted in malpractice action. Nevertheless, there's a gray zone in microscopic and X-ray interpretation that must be recognized (see Chapter 42). Unfortunately, a great many malpractice cases fall in this gray zone. Only hindsight reveals seemingly obvious errors. Charges of malpractice in these instances are understandable, but there must be a consensus of interpretation before failure to diagnose becomes a reasonable charge. Too many malpractice suits appear to be based on hindsight, with too little consideration of the circumstances existing at the time of the incident.

In reviewing hundreds of patients' records in cases where diagnostic failure was charged, I found conditions misdiagnosed (or undiagnosed) in the following order of frequency:

1. Breast cancer
2. Lung cancer
3. Appendicitis
4. Blunt upper abdominal trauma
5. Uterus: cervix, then fundus cancer
6. Ovarian cancer
7. Colon (excluding rectal) cancer
8. Stomach cancer
9. Mouth cancer.

The sine qua non of good medical practice is accurate diagnosis. When diagnosis remains in doubt, it's difficult to proceed with therapy. The critical importance of correct diagnosis is recognized by patient and physician alike, but its emotional focus lies with the patient, who wants his questions answered and fears allayed. When questions go unanswered, anxiety builds and, with it, hostility: "That stupid doctor can't even figure out what's wrong with me!" It's easy to see why so many malpractice suits arise in this kind of climate.

Should the patient die without a firm diagnosis, an autopsy is the best way to clarify the esoteric nature of his condition and to support your position with regard to the medical issues involved. But get permission from the proper relative. Doing a postmortem with permission from the wrong relative subjects you to liability just as much as if you were doing it without permission from anyone.

Who's the right person to give permission for an autopsy? If the patient has reached his majority, his own signed permission is all that's needed. Next on the list is the surviving spouse. She loses her place in line, however, if she wasn't married to the deceased at the time of his death. If such is the case, or if there is no surviving spouse, consent of the adult children—preferably all of them—must be obtained.

If the deceased is an unmarried adult or a minor, parental permission is needed. Although the law isn't clear about which parent you must ask, it would appear that the father is first choice. However, it's best not to take chances, so try to obtain permission from both parents. If the parents are divorced or separated, consent of the one who has custody of the child is adequate.

At times it isn't known whether the deceased had any family, or how to contact the family. It would be best then to pass up the autopsy. The coroner's office in occasional instances may be of some help. In that event it becomes a "coroner's case." However, when you're sure the deceased had no immediate family and no other relatives attended his last illness, you're probably safe in proceeding. If a second cousin does show up later, he'll have a tough time proving that the autopsy caused him any mental anguish.

Even after consent has been obtained from the right relative, an autopsy isn't entirely free of risk. One must keep strictly to the terms of the consent. The person who consents may restrict his permission as to place, as to manner, and, most important, as to extent. Generally, permission to conduct an autopsy does not give one the right to remove an organ permanently. For that you need specific consent.

The courts recognize the right of an individual to control the disposition of his own body after death. Provisions authorizing an autopsy have been upheld in wills, releases, and insurance policies. They are becoming more frequent, especially in relation to the donation of specific organs.

3

Defensive medicine

It's obvious to the practicing physician in today's litigious society that the areas in which he's exposed to malpractice charges are protean. Can he make his practice more malpractice-proof? The answers are assuredly not simple; no dogmatic conclusions should be drawn. One method, which undoubtedly owes much to the wave of consumerism and redress to the courts, is to resort to defensive medicine.

How widespread is such practice among U.S. doctors? The Department of Health, Education, and Welfare's Commission on Medical Malpractice,[1] in its landmark 1973 report, concluded that the extent to which defensive medicine is practiced was not known. In a 1978 survey reported in Business Week, 75 percent of the respondents admitted to practicing defensive medicine.[2] And a Medical Economics study[3] established that if you are like the great majority of your colleagues, you're doing certain things to protect yourself.

Much more important than the extent of defensive medicine is the question whether it's good for doctors and patients. The survey pinpoints some healthy practice changes around the country and also some disturbing ones.

It's to the nation's benefit that a good many doctors are now more thorough about diagnostic testing—but not beneficial that quite a few doctors order unnecessary tests simply for self-protection. It's laudable that a considerable number are keeping more complete patient records—but not laudable that some add many nonessentials merely for legal show.

Similarly, some doctors have become commendably cautious about allowing prescription refills; others allow none at all, making the patient come in and pay for an office visit whenever he wants any sort of prescription renewal. While some are more judicious about referring tricky cases to appropriate specialists, others are unloading even cases they're fully qualified to handle if they see any possibility of an untoward result.

Overall, the malpractice-inspired changes may have improved standards of care, but often with a loss of efficiency and a rise in costs. These are the very factors that spur agitation in Washington for more controls. Therefore, you have to weigh your risks against your patients' circumstances in deciding how far to go with malpractice-proofing.

To let you judge your own actions in the light of what your colleagues are doing, detailed questionnaires were sent to a random national sample of 4,020 practicing physicians, of whom 35 per cent responded.[3] They were asked whether concern about legal liability had led them to make any of 15 specified practice changes, from getting more consultations and hospitalizing more patients to giving patients more information about risks. Over 80 per cent checked at least one. Table 3-1 shows the results.

Did responses come mostly from doctors who had been burned by malpractice? On the contrary. Only three in 10 respondents had

Table 3-1

How malpractice-proofing options rank

Practice change	Per cent
Order more diagnostic tests	48
Tell patients more about risks	44
Keep more detailed patient records	44
Use more consultations	40
Allow fewer prescription refills	37
Refer more cases	31
Give less telephone advice	31
Stop performing certain procedures	30
Accept new patients more selectively	25
Schedule more follow-up visits	24
Use consent forms for more procedures	20
Hospitalize more cases	18
Stick closer to recommended drug dosages	17
Take more extensive initial histories	16
Delegate fewer procedures	14
Take additional steps	7

been subjected even to threats of suit. Only two in 10 had had formal claims filed against them, and only one in 10 had been in litigation.

Many respondents also elaborated on the changes they've made for malpractice protection. These are listed as "additional steps" in Table 3-1. Measures included prescribing new drugs of doubtful value, done by a psychiatrist eager to prove he was up on the latest therapy, and omitting mention of problems in surgical reports, done by a surgeon to avoid questioning by patients' attorneys. Most of these respondents, however, described specific steps they were taking to build sounder relationships with patients.

It's been charged that we've gone too far in practicing defensive medicine. Cost containment has become a watchword among legislators all over the United States. Health Systems Agencies decide who may and who may not install expensive diagnostic equipment such as CAT scanners. In an effort to prevent unnecessary surgery, Blue Shield and about 100 commercial carriers will pay for second opinions in certain cases. And Blue Cross has proposed not to pay for batteries of tests routinely performed on hospital admission.

How far these measures will affect the quality of health care in the United States is unknown. Certainly, though, they'll place a premium on the essentials of sound medical care: our education, training, judgment, and dedication. And as we retrench, it'll be increasingly important to educate, inform, and maintain rapport with patients.

References

1. *Medical Malpractice: Report of the Secretary's Commission on Medical Malpractice.* Washington, DC: U.S. Department of Health, Education, and Welfare, publication No. (OS) 73-88, 1973
2. Unhealthy costs of health. *Business Week,* Sept 4, 1978, p 58
3. *Making Your Practice More Malpractice Proof.* Oradell, NJ: Medical Economics Book Division, 1973

4

Abandonment and follow-up examinations

Abandonment suits against physicians have quadrupled over the past decade. Bigger patient loads are probably part of the reason; they make it harder for a doctor to give any one patient immediate attention. But there's another reason: Many doctors don't know exactly what constitutes abandonment.

Abandonment has been defined by one court as "a failure by the physician to continue to provide service to the patient when it is still needed in a case for which the physician has assumed responsibility and from which he has not been properly relieved." Therefore, when a doctor doesn't respond to a patient's demand for medical attention, he's abandoning the patient in a legal sense if two factors are present: (1) The patient must have a genuine need for the attention he demands, and (2) a previously created relationship between doctor and patient must be in effect when the demand for treatment occurs.

Suppose a woman finds your name in the telephone directory and calls you at midnight. Her husband, she says frantically, is seriously ill. You rush to the bedside. You see him again in a few days and find that he's recovered. Months later, while you're out on hospital calls, your office reaches you to report that the same woman wants you to visit her husband again. You feel that your first duty is to your regular patients, so you tell your secretary to suggest another physician. While the woman is trying to reach the second doctor, her husband dies. Are you vulnerable to charges of abandonment?

Probably not, if you've taken certain precautions. The first of the two conditions exists: The patient's need is real. But the second, your continuing responsibility toward him, is doubtful. The relationship you establish with the patient is self-limiting if you tell him your treatment will end when he recovers and if you show completion of his treatment in your records. Thus your implied contract with them is no longer in force when you're asked to make the later visit. You then have as much right to refuse your services as you would have with a new patient.

A court might conceivably rule otherwise because laws vary from state to state and the courts' interpretations of those laws aren't always predictable. Yet the principles underlying the abandonment statutes are universal, and their proper application is often a matter of common sense. If you know what the laws allow, and if you follow them, you have little to fear even if a suit-prone patient does take you to court for abandonment. You also minimize the risk of bad publicity that merely being accused can cause: the melodramatic picture of a callous doctor deserting a patient in need of care.

Patients' rights and physicians' responsibilities aren't always as clear-cut as the simple definition of abandonment might suggest. They are affected by circumstances. Below are some other situations that illustrate how the principles apply:

Postoperative care. Dr. A is a busy general surgeon. Before discharging a patient from the hospital after an operation, he reminds her of his previous advice to visit her family doctor for postoperative check-ups. What if the patient fails to follow his advice and lands in the hospital again as the result of a complication?

The surgeon is within his rights. He isn't responsible for postoperative care if he has advised the patient beforehand that he is unable to or does not intend to undertake such care. This is unlikely during hospitalization. Once the patient is discharged, however, it is not an uncommon practice.

Any specialist may decline to give treatment outside his specialty. A general practitioner, specialist in family practice, or internist may say he'll see patients only at his office. All doctors can limit their practices. If they tell their patients about such restrictions, their refusal to exceed the limitations is not abandonment. Nevertheless, here's a situation that illustrates an important exception:

Infant care. Dr. B is a board-certified obstetrician. She sent a patient home from the hospital with her baby after a normal delivery. She then left for vacation without ascertaining whether the parents had called the pediatrician whose name she had supplied at their request. What if the child gets sick and dies?

The obstetrician may be open to abandonment charges. The rule that doctors can accept or refuse patients doesn't apply to infants they have delivered. Their responsibility is especially grave if they suspect a congenital illness or observe a birth injury or defect. They must provide continuous care of an infant patient until certain that another physician has taken over.

Emergency care. Dr. C is a general practitioner. A woman who tripped on the sidewalk is brought to his office. He applies a temporary splint to her broken arm and tells her to go to an orthopedist to have the fracture set. What if she disregards his instructions and develops a deformity requiring corrective surgery?

The doctor is on dangerous footing. He can be considered to have committed abandonment by making the patient responsible for ensuring that another practitioner will provide further care. To be safe, he should make certain that another doctor will carry on where he leaves off. Equally serious, and similar, are the risks a doctor runs if he fails to follow up on a patient he has seen while on emergency room duty.

The cancer patient or a potential cancer patient. This is a critical area for both patient and physician, and one where good rapport between the two is essential. Theoretically, a cancer patient should never be discharged. The responsibility for follow-up must be assumed by one or another of the physicians on the case, whether the original, primary physician or the treating specialist or group of specialists. The same may be said, though in a more discretionary sense, concerning a patient who has a problem that could be or could lead to the development of cancer. Regularly scheduled visits and re-examinations, wisely spaced but not too far apart, and then recorded in the patient's chart, are necessary; nothing less is considered acceptable.

Protect yourself against abandonment charges by following these six rules:

1. If you intend to limit your services in any way, say so before you start treatment. This rule includes any refusal to treat under Medicare or Medicaid. To be safe, state your limitation in writing or in the presence of a witness other than your office assistant.

2. When advising patients that treatment is completed, let your office records indicate the reason. If a patient has recovered or reached a point where further treatment wouldn't materially improve his condition, make a notation to that effect.

3. If you want to drop a patient for nonpayment of medical bills or for other reasons, such as refusal to accept your advice, making unreasonable demands, or consistently breaking appointments, send him a registered letter with return receipt requested. Offer to remain available for a reasonable time, during which the patient can find another physician. If the patient needs further medical care, inform him fully and keep a record of the advice you give him.

4. When a patient dismisses you, send him a letter confirming the break in your relationship and keep a copy on file.

5. If you know you're going to be out of town, have your office assistant notify all patients who are acutely ill, convalescing from operations, pregnant, or subject to chronic disorders. Make available to them or give them the name, address, and telephone number of a competent physician who has agreed to cover for you.

6. Make sure that any decision to deny a patient's request for attention or further follow-up care is based on medical judgment. Courts have often ruled that you cannot refuse to treat a patient merely because you are occupied with other patients. A consultation with another doctor will often substantiate the reason for denial of further services or closer follow-up attention.

5

You and your staff

A West Coast doctor's office assistant gave a patient a vitamin injection. When the patient suffered a wristdrop, she sued the doctor. The court, noting that such a result should not ordinarily follow a routine injection unless negligently performed, held that it was up to the doctor to prove there had been no negligence.

That would not have been easy. The assistant wasn't a registered nurse and therefore wasn't licensed by the state to give injections. No matter how deft she might be with the needle and syringe, legally she was not qualified. The case was settled without further court proceedings.

Delegating paramedical responsibilities to well-trained assistants is customary in doctors' offices throughout the United States. The practice is increasing as the number of licensed physicians' assistants and nurse practitioners grows. Yet the custom has its risks for the individual physician. In many states, it's dangerous for a doctor to let an office or hospital assistant perform any medical or surgical function unless the assistant is specifically licensed to do so.

That conclusion is implicit in a decision handed down by the California supreme court as long ago as December 1961. The case involved the chief anesthesiologist of a hospital who employed three graduate physicians to assist him in giving anesthesia, including spinal and epidural. All three doctors were trained and experienced anesthesiologists, but none was licensed to practice medicine in California.

In employing them the doctor had acted in good faith. His attorney advised him that it was perfectly legal. Yet the California Board of Medical Examiners charged him with violation of the state law, which forbids employing or "aiding and abetting" an unlicensed person to practice medicine. The board found him guilty of unprofessional conduct and revoked his license.

The physician appealed to the courts. Eventually, the California supreme court agreed with the medical examiners that he was guilty of unprofessional conduct. It found, though, that taking away his license was too severe a penalty.

In its decision, the court concluded that the administration of anesthetics "is obviously an integral part of the surgical treatment which it facilitates." It pointed out that by statutory exceptions, students, interns, and teachers at approved hospitals and registered nurses under the immediate direction and supervision of a licensed physician may do certain things that constitute treatment of the sick. However, in the absence of such statutory exception, said the court, anyone not licensed to practice medicine or surgery cannot legally perform medical or surgical acts. A doctor who aids and abets an unauthorized person to do so "is guilty of unprofessional conduct . . . even though the acts are done under his immediate direction and supervision."

The court then considered whether revocation of the anesthesiologist's license was justified. The doctor, said the court, "was confronted with a question not specifically answered by the code or by any decision of our courts. . . . 'Suspending judgment' or 'placing him on probation,' as permitted by the code, would be a more appropriate discipline, and the case should be returned to the board for reconsideration of the penalty to be imposed." The board did reconsider. It restored the physician's license and placed him on probation for three years.

The court's decision could mean that physicians in other states with similar licensing codes are not able to employ assistants for medical or surgical tasks, such as injections, unless the assistants are specifically authorized by law to perform them. Otherwise, such physicians would be breaking the law even though they closely supervised the assistants.

Although not widely publicized at that time, the California decision has influenced legal interpretations in states with similar medical practice acts. It also explains the proliferation of ancillary and paramedical personnel trained and educated for specific purposes. The increased cost to physician and hospital is obvious, but it's justified in terms of time saved and the availability of expertise.

Medicolegal experts believe the California decision might well be echoed by the courts in a number of states: Arkansas, Colorado, Louisiana, Texas, and Washington, among others. In Washington, as in a number of other jurisdictions, changing dressings and giving injections fall clearly within the legal definition of the practice of medicine. Such procedures may be done only by a licensed practitioner or a registered nurse under his direction. Yet in numerous doctors' offices assistants who aren't registered nurses are doing this work. The doctors who let them may be breaking the law.

The medical practice acts are far less clear-cut in many other states. Minnesota is one where the legalities of delegating are vague and uncertain. "On the basis of cases that have been decided in Minnesota," says one attorney, "it's hard to tell just what medical procedures may legally be performed by someone who is not a licensed physician. A doctor should be most conservative in deciding which procedure he will permit a nurse or a technician to do under his supervision."

The law appears even more indefinite in South Dakota, with no statutes or court decisions on delegation. Other states where the vagueness of the law indicates caution include Hawaii, Illinois, Michigan, New York, and Vermont. The laws of Illinois and New York not only fail to deal specifically with delegation, they don't even define medical practice. This legal area is still open to court decisions that could do professional damage to doctors.

Whether the laws are vague or explicit, in today's sophisticated medical environment many physicians cannot avoid delegating some paramedical duties to assistants who may not be specifically licensed. In addition to increasing the efficiency and quality of medical care, paramedical personnel lighten the burden of the "overworked" physician so that he may apply his full efforts and training to the more urgent aspects of his practice. Their essential function demands that the physician be highly select not only in employing them but in delegating authority that inevitably will reflect on him. Follow these five simple but worthwhile precautions:

1. Make sure the assistants you hire are intelligent and dependable. Check thoroughly on their background and experience.

2. Provide your assistants with whatever additional formal training is available. Make use of courses given by the local county and state medical societies.

3. Be certain your assistants understand what to do, how to do it, and why. Be explicit.

4. Spell out for your assistants the limitations of their jobs. Provide definite guidelines.

5. Impress your assistants with the importance of calling to your attention anything about which they have doubts. Maintain easy communication with all of your staff.

6

You and your hospital

Some nautical-minded judge long ago decided that there was a similarity between a surgeon in the operating room and the master of a windjammer. Both had absolute authority "on board" and should bear equal responsibility if something went wrong. Each was captain of his ship. More recently, some judges have disagreed with this principle. They have recognized that although a surgeon has great responsibility, he doesn't hire hospital personnel or buy hospital supplies. In today's complex medical world, he's dependent on the presumed expertise of other individuals. There are times, however, when this expertise may be lacking.

The legal responsibility of a physician to his hospitalized patients does not begin and end with his own acts or omissions. In the first place, hospital rules may place the burden of responsibility for an employee's act on the shoulders of the attending physician or surgeon in certain circumstances. Even if the rules are not so interpreted, the plaintiff in a malpractice suit might still manage to convince the jury that you had "control" of the employee when negligence occurred.

Obviously you can't foresee or prevent all the mishaps that might possibly take place when a patient is hospitalized. You can, however, be alert to several commonly encountered situations that pose potential problems for you.

Anesthetic accidents. When an anesthetic accident occurs, states one medicolegal expert, "the plaintiff's lawyer tends to sue everyone in sight, regardless of the medical and surgical disciplines involved."

That's what happened in the case of a 49-year-old woman who was scheduled to undergo a vaginoplasty. After being administered a spinal anesthetic, the patient suffered cardiac arrest. A thoracotomy was quickly performed and her heart massaged, but spontaneous breathing did not resume for almost an hour. In the meantime she was given oxygen under pressure.

Present while this was going on were the surgeon, the anesthesiologist on the case, two residents assisting them, and, part of the time, the hospital's chief of anesthesiology plus another staff anesthesiologist. The doctors' efforts saved the woman's life, but she suffered permanent and disabling brain damage. When the extent of her injury became evident, the woman's husband sued the hospital and all six physicians.

The trial was a debacle for the defendants. Although several of the doctors had helped with the anesthesia and resuscitation, it wasn't clear who had actually given the spinal injection. The operating surgeon claimed he didn't know. No one could explain a chart entry stating that the anesthetic agent, a mixture of tetracaine and epinephrine, had been injected at what was called the "unexplainably high level" of T-10!

Such confusing testimony persuaded the defendants to settle rather than let the case go to the jury. The price of medical confusion came high. While the two residents and the staff anesthesiologist were released from liability, the remaining three doctors were not, nor was the hospital.

The accident might have been avoided if the surgeon had insisted on conferring with the anesthesiologist and the residents before the operation. A discussion of the type of anesthesia, its extent and degree, and the nature of the operation contemplated is simply good medical practice. Nothing less should be considered acceptable.

Transfusion mishaps. An attending physician can be held liable if his patient gets the wrong blood despite the fact that the error is caused by an employee of the hospital.

A 25-year-old woman was admitted to a hospital for treatment of a ureteral stone. A 5-mm calculus was caught in the distal third of the right ureter and causing obstruction. The kidney, damaged previously from a congenital kink at the upper end of the ureter, was poorly functioning and in danger of further destruction.

The woman's attending urologist performed a pyeloplasty to remove the kink from the ureter and a nephrostomy to provide drainage for the kidney. Before the operation he ordered a pint of blood to be made available for transfusion. The blood was not used and was sent back to the hospital blood bank.

When subsequent attempts to remove the stone by cystoscopy failed, the doctor scheduled a second operation. Because he expected the operation would be brief, he ordered no blood this time.

Shortly before the operation was to start, a circulating nurse in the operating room and employed by the hospital found a note on her desk saying, "The patient's blood is in the refrigerator." She wrongly assumed that the blood was for the woman in the operating room and gave the blood to the nurse anesthetist on the case, an employee of the hospital anesthesiologist.

The operation, as often may happen, turned out to be more extensive than anticipated. In the course of it the anesthetist asked the surgeon, "Doctor, I have a pint of blood for this patient. Shall I give it to her now?"

Assuming that this was the blood he had ordered for the first operation, the doctor replied, "Yes, give it to her." Ten hours later she was dead.

Not long afterward her husband, left with two infant children, brought suit. He named the surgeon, the hospital as the employer of the circulating nurse who had made the initial error, and the anesthesiologist, who was not even present at the operation but was the employer of the nurse anesthetist who had failed to discover the error.

A jury found all three defendants liable. It reasoned that although the surgeon was not responsible for the error, he knew he had not specifically ordered blood for the second operation and should have been aware of this. To quote one of the trial lawyers, "If the doctor had said, 'What blood? I didn't order any blood,' we would not be here in court."

"Wrong patient" cases. These are costly mistakes. They will occur when a number of people, including the surgeon, ignore a series of hospital rules designed to prevent such errors. An illustrative case occurred in Michigan. Five individuals ignored five separate rules, and a patient whose injured hand was to have been repaired had a kidney removed instead.

It started when the operating room orderly handed a floor nurse a slip of paper on which was written the name of a patient scheduled for a kidney operation. Instead of taking the orderly to the correct bed and patient, the nurse pointed to a room and said, "The patient is in bed number two."

Entering the ward, the orderly went to what he thought was bed number two. Unfortunately, he began counting beds from the wrong end of the row and, therefore, got the wrong patient. He ignored a hospital regulation that states orderlies must always check the patient's bed card.

The operating room supervisor made the third mistake. Although she was required to verify the identity of every patient who entered the surgical suite, she failed to do it for this patient. She was very busy and merely told the orderly, "Put the patient on the operating table."

The anesthesiologist kept the ball rolling. He should ask each patient, "What is your name?" and inspect the patient's wrist band for identification. Instead, he uttered the reassuring words "Just take a few deep breaths and you'll soon be sound asleep."

The surgeon himself made the final mistake. The hospital rules said he must identify all his patients before they are anesthetized. But he arrived in the operating room late. When he found the patient already asleep, he went ahead and operated.

The patient and the surgeon wound up as the sole victims of this morbid chain of circumstances. The patient decided to sue only the surgeon. The surgeon settled.

Is it unlikely that any such mix-up can occur in your hospital? Yes, but it was also unlikely to occur in the usually well-run institution where it did. And as long as one person after another gets careless and breaks the rules, similar incidents will continue to happen in otherwise well-run institutions. You can never take for granted that the system is working.

Accidents caused by careless hospital employees under a doctor's supervision. A Colorado surgeon was certain he couldn't be held liable for an operating room accident. He felt that the nurse anesthetist had been negligent and the orderly thoughtless. He was confident the jury would see where the fault lay as soon as it knew the full facts.

The patient had been on the operating room table when the surgeon entered the room. The nurse anesthetist was at the patient's head and an orderly at the foot of the table. The surgeon told the orderly to place the patient on his side, and the orderly obeyed.

Turning to have his gown tied, the doctor told the orderly to strap the patient. But when the orderly left the table to get a strap, the patient fell and was injured. The patient sued the surgeon.

The doctor's defense was as follows: (1) The patient was in the charge of the nurse anesthetist and the orderly when the accident occurred; (2) the orderly was a hospital employee over whom the surgeon exercised no control; and (3) the nurse anesthetist was an independent contractor whose services were paid for by the patient through his hospital bill. In light of these clear facts, could anyone consider the doctor liable?

The jury could, and did.

The court, in upholding the jury's verdict, pointed out that the nurse anesthetist could not have been expected to give full attention to the patient since it was her duty to administer an anesthetic and observe related vital signs. The doctor, by giving a specific order to the orderly, had assumed command and responsibility. He had, therefore, been negligent in telling the orderly to do something that would leave the patient momentarily unattended.

In another case, an Oklahoma surgeon had told an operating room nurse to remove a dressing and clean a child's skin in preparation for reducing an open, compound fracture of the clavicle. After the fracture was reduced and the cast applied, the doctor noticed that the child's skin was red and irritated. Later, when the cast was removed, there was a skin burn from the anterior shoulder to the small of the back. Fortunately, the wound had healed.

In the suit that followed, the surgeon alone was held liable for the accident. True, the nurse was a hospital employee, but she had worked under the doctor's supervision. Doing so, she became his "borrowed" employee. Her negligence in applying the antiseptic that burned the child's skin, which the surgeon should have observed, was essentially his responsibility.

In protecting yourself against liability in the hospital, bear in mind that it is not only a patient who might sue you; the hospital itself might do so. As the shield of charitable immunity has been withdrawn from hospitals, their malpractice burden has grown accordingly. Inevitably, some hospitals have tended to shift the onus of responsibility to the physician. A malpractice suit in New York is case in point.

A woman sued both her obstetrician and the hospital, claiming she had developed a postpartum infection, high fever, and other complications of childbirth. She charged the hospital with negligence in failing to sterilize instruments, using unclean needles, employing unskilled personnel, and letting her stay in a soiled bed. The doctor was charged with improperly diagnosing and treating the complications and with allowing her to be placed in a soiled bed.

Before the woman's suit came to trial, the hospital cross-claimed against the codefendant physician, arguing that if there had been any negligence, his was active while its own was passive. The court threw out the cross-complaint. It reasoned that when two parties are charged with separate acts of negligence, neither party can shift his liability to his codefendant. The court's decision held up on appeal.

Suppose, however, that the patient's suit names only the hospital. In this situation, ironically, the physician apparently has less chance of having the hospital's cross-complaint dismissed than he would have as a codefendant. A good example is another case in New York.

The patient claimed a nerve had been severed during a thyroidectomy, making her hoarse. She sued the hospital and the resident who had performed the operation. The hospital's third-party complaint brought in the attending surgeon (who had supervised), as well as the anesthesiologist. The court turned down the surgeon's motion to dismiss the hospital's charge.

Unlike the first case cited above, where each codefendant was charged with separate acts of negligence, this one involved a single act: the severing of a nerve. Thus the only issue, the court ruled, was who was responsible for this act.

Sometimes a hospital that has lost a negligence case will try to force a doctor to pay part of the award. In one such case the trial court, finding both surgeon and hospital guilty, awarded a patient $22,500 for injuries from a postoperative intravenous injection. The appellate court later reversed the judgment against the doctor, saying he had a right to rely on the hospital staff to administer the injection properly. At this point the patient agreed to a reduced settlement of $17,500. The hospital appealed, claiming that the surgeon's insurance company should pay part of the award because the trial court had found the doctor guilty. But the state's highest court dismissed the appeal, pointing out that the appellate court had already cleared the doctor.

The best way to prevent a clash between the hospital and its medical staff over malpractice liability is through collective action by the staff. It has the power to remove colleagues whose careless ways will increase the hospital's malpractice rate. It also has the power to persuade hospital officials to cooperate with the physician in malpractice defense.

Section II

Clinical studies and review

The chapters that follow contain case studies emphasizing specific areas of exposure to malpractice. The mere occurrence of something untoward is not necessarily malpractice. Nonetheless, anything less than a reasonably good result raises the question of liability. Paramount is the question of acceptability: Was an acceptable standard of care maintained? If so, it's difficult to substantiate the charge of malpractice in court.

These case reviews illustrate highly variant standards of care. Specific interpretation of liability in many of these cases may be a matter of opinion. The medical-surgical problems, on the other hand, are not. The clinical areas of vulnerability to malpractice are readily apparent.

The practicing physician learns best by clinical example. That's why case studies are so necessary. Each case study is a compilation of numerous similar cases put together to form a clinical subject for review. The case reports were, in a sense, synthesized to present general problems commonly encountered by physicians. The discussions accompanying the case reports reflect my own opinions. These opinions, like any others, are subject to debate.*

*All cases are completely anonymous (see Introduction).

7

The head and neck

Head and neck mishaps are a leading cause of wrongful death actions. From a dollars-and-cents viewpoint they're generally regarded as lesser malpractice risks. Typically, the deceased patient is a child, and, as one trial lawyer has put it bluntly, "Children die cheap." This attitude, however, is changing.

A $10,000 or $15,000 verdict, though limited, cannot reflect what the death of a child does to a physician, to his practice, or to the public image of the medical profession in the community in which it occurs. So it's important to have a clear idea of the leading medicolegal risks in the area of the mouth, pharynx, and larynx as well as the neck itself.

Post-tonsillectomy hemorrhage. A T&A is one of the most technically underrated operations. Post-tonsillectomy hemorrhage is the basis of all too many recorded malpractice cases. The lesson to be derived from each is: When you do a tonsillectomy, take stringent steps to prevent postoperative hemorrhage.

The physician being sued is usually at fault for one of two reasons: Either he performed too many operations in a limited period to save time, doing what plaintiffs' lawyers call "mass-production surgery," or he left the hospital with undue haste after performing the surgery. Postoperative recovery room care doesn't let the surgeon off the hook; he must be at hand or available in case complications develop.

One New York surgeon had the reputation of doing the fastest T&As in town. He'd get his patients out of the hospital so quickly that they had hardly anything about the operation to tell their friends. A 10-year-old patient of his never got even that much chance. Her story was finally told, but in courtroom prose, when her parents sued the surgeon for malpractice and wrongful death.

The patient had been a bright, active girl, and the plaintiff's lawyer didn't have to work hard to collect a verdict. The surgeon admitted, "I must have operated on about 12 children that morning." When the girl's fatal hemorrhage started, he was operating on another patient in another hospital and so couldn't come to her immediately.

The girl's need should have been "reasonably anticipated," the jurors decided. They refused to consider the doctor's excuse that he was busy doing an operation at another hospital. They obviously didn't like the fact that he had scheduled that morning's surgery en masse to suit his own convenience.

A jury likes it even less if a doctor leaves a postoperative patient prematurely so that he can get to his office. To be legally safe, you should stay at the hospital with a patient until your medical judgment tells you it's all right to leave or until you've made arrangements for a surgeon to cover in case of hemorrhage. The fact that there's a roomful of sick people waiting at your office is no excuse for breaking this rule.

Assault and battery in pharyngeal surgery. This medicolegal risk in T&A cases carries a simple lesson: Keep within the operative consent.

A settlement is difficult to avoid if a doctor is charged with removing a patient's adenoids when the operative consent covers only a tonsillectomy. An East Coast surgeon performed such an unauthorized "favor" for a young patient referred to him by a general practitioner for a tonsillectomy. The surgeon had assumed out of habit that a T&A was called for. Wisely, he went along with a small "nuisance" settlement and agreed not to bill the vindictive parents for the operation.

Perforation of the esophagus during a bronchoscopy. This injury may be serious and can result in death. The price can run into six figures. One plaintiff's attorney recently collected a large sum for the wrongful death of a 40-year-old man with a wife and two children. Another lawyer had to take less, perhaps because the patient had been 62.

Except for the dollar amounts paid, the two cases were much the same. In each, a doctor without sufficient experience tried to force a bronchoscope into his patient's pharynx. Each perforated the esophagus, causing a cervical abscess followed by a fatal mediastinitis. Such a mishap is less likely to occur in the hands of an experienced endoscopist. Bronchial endoscopy requires special training.

Failure to detect cancer of the larynx. This malpractice charge is common. Two facts underscore why it has become a serious risk for practitioners.

First, the risk cuts across all types of practices. Whatever his specialty, if a doctor looks in a patient's throat or hears a complaint of hoarseness, he's a potential candidate for this type of trouble. Second, cancer suits are increasingly popular with plaintiffs' attorneys who specialize in malpractice cases.

One malpractice case that ended in a large settlement involved a patient who had continually complained of hoarseness to his physician. The complaint never seemed severe enough to indicate a need for consultation, hospitalization, or surgery. Because the man was a heavy cigarette smoker, his internist told him to cut down to a pack a day! The man followed that advice, but continued his complaints when his voice didn't improve. Finally, after three years, he went to an otolaryngologist, only to learn that his larynx was cancerous and would have to be removed. The day he was discharged from the hospital, he called on his attorney.

The internist hadn't suspected cancer, and it probably wasn't present all those years. But three years of complaints about hoarseness should have made a consultation mandatory. The doctor was forced to settle out of court.

A case such as this warns us of the diagnostic capriciousness of head and neck cancer. There is an increasing number of lawsuits related to this difficult anatomical area, all alleging failure to make a timely diagnosis of cancer. For both physician and patient the head and neck can be one of the most frustrating diagnostic sites in the body. In addition to this, it's an area that frequently demands the ultimate in surgical skill. The many lawsuits related to the thyroid and major salivary glands are substantial proof of this fact.

8

Oropharyngeal cancer: Waldeyer's ring

A 64-year-old man consulted his family physician because of a sore throat of two weeks' duration. There were no other complaints, and he was able to swallow without much pain or difficulty. He smoked about three packs of cigarettes a day; he was a moderately heavy drinker. Examination with a tongue depressor revealed only a mildly infected pharynx, more so on the right. There were no enlarged lymph nodes in the neck. Oral antibiotics were prescribed along with a throat gargle. There was slight improvement of symptoms. The patient's smoking and drinking habits remained unchanged.

Over the ensuing seven months, the throat soreness continued, waxing and waning as the patient was switched from one antibiotic to another, but never truly subsiding. Swallowing became slightly more painful. Examinations of his throat with a tongue depressor alone were continued and always reported to be unremarkable.

Eight months following the patient's first visit, he was referred to a specialist in otorhinolaryngology, who on careful indirect laryngoscopy (mirror) and then on direct laryngoscopy found some leukoplakia along the right lateral pharyngeal wall just behind the right anterior tonsillar pillar. This was the only physical finding, and the specialist felt there was nothing to biopsy. The neck was negative for enlarged lymph nodes. A subsequent examination one month later showed no changes and "nothing remarkable."

Since the soreness continued, the patient consulted another ENT specialist three months later. At this time there was an obvious ulcerating cancer occupying the right anterior tonsillar pillar, the right glossopalatine fold, and the right base of the tongue with extension to the right lateral pharyngeal wall. There was an enlarged, 2-cm lymph node in the right subdigastric area. Biopsy of the tumor at a site on the right anterior tonsillar pillar was positive for squamous cell carcinoma, moderately well differentiated.

Supravoltage radiation therapy was given to both the primary site and the enlarged lymph node. The patient refused surgery, and no neck dissection was performed.[1] Recurrences were manifest within 10 months both at the primary site and also by additional right cervical lymph node metastases. Chemotherapy with methotrexate was of little help; the patient died of cancer two years and eight months following the initial visit to his family physician. Suit was filed against the family physician, alleging that failure to make a timely diagnosis of cancer of the throat led to the patient's death.

Discussion and comment. The occult nature of cancer of the oropharynx is common knowledge. It's almost axiomatic that in some patients such cancers will defy detection until too late to cure.[2-5] Does accumulated experience[5,6] mitigate exposure for the physician in this case? The fact that both the patient's family physician and an ENT specialist could not, on careful examination, elicit a positive finding that suggested the presence of cancer can only attest to the occult nature of this disease.

Ultimately the cancer will break through at the primary site or become highly suggestive by virtue of an enlarged cervical lymph node metastasis.[7,8] The exposure to malpractice charges is understandable from the lay standpoint ("Why, the cancer was there all the time!"), but certainly not from the medical point of view. How, then, could the physician have protected himself?

Examination of a patient who complains of a sore throat month after month demands more than a tongue depressor. When the findings or signs don't fit the symptoms, an early consultation is warranted. When antibiotics are not helpful after a two-week trial, neoplasia should be a paramount consideration. When leukoplakia is persistent and accompanied by a history of heavy tobacco use with alcohol, the occult areas of the oropharynx and hypopharynx (anterior tonsillar pillar, glossopalatine fold, lateral pharyngeal wall, base of the tongue, and vallecula, i.e., Waldeyer's ring) should be especially considered, and perhaps a blind biopsy or, at least, excision of the area of leukoplakia should be performed.[5,6,9] Action is understandably a matter of judgment, but in this case much in the clinical picture and history was suggestive of cancer.

The patient died of cancer arising in the general anatomical area termed the oropharynx or hypopharynx. Since he was a heavy smoker and drinker, there's little question that his tissues in this region, if biopsied at various sites, would have revealed many of the histologic signs of cellular atypism and also multiple sites of origin of hypopharyngeal or oropharyngeal cancer. These small, scattered nests of cancer and collections of atypism probably smoldered for a while and ultimately became biologically aggressive, extended outward, coalesced with other small nests, and formed one large cancer.[2,10] All this can happen in a surprisingly short time, so that on one examination the area is clinically negative and only three months later it's clinically obvious for cancer.

This chain of events, which happens in the oropharyngeal tissues of many patients, explains why the cancer was clinically indeterminable, or occult, in its early stages.[11] Diagnosis in this incipient phase was very likely impossible or, at best, barely feasible. Even with repeated, blind biopsies, unless the physician had been lucky enough to select an area containing a nest of cancer cells, the true nature of the process would still have remained hidden. By the time the small nests of cancer joined to form one big cancer, it could fairly be considered too late to be cured.[10] Therefore, there's little question that liability was limited.

Even if this cancer had been diagnosed and treated early, it probably would soon have broken out nearby. This pattern is often termed a "cancer diathesis" and is all too frequently seen with oropharyngeal cancers: As soon as one area of cancer is cured, a neighboring site breaks out.

This case is a frustrating example of how the disease itself, because of difficulty in diagnosis and a predictably poor prognosis, enhances the physician's exposure to malpractice. That exposure was abetted by the medical failures and omissions discussed above.

The only way the physician could have refuted charges of failure to diagnose, which unhappily are always made on hindsight, would have been to pursue an aggressive (and often costly) diagnostic regimen. In some circles this is called defensive medicine.

References

1. Jesse RH, Lindberg RD: The efficacy of combining radiation therapy with a surgical procedure in patients with cervical metastases from squamous cancer of the oropharynx and hypopharynx. *Cancer* 35:1163, 1975
2. Bauer WC: Varieties of squamous carcinoma: Biologic behavior. *Front Radiat Ther Oncol* 9:164, 1974
3. Gilbert H, Kagan AR: Recurrence patterns in squamous cell carcinoma of the oral cavity, pharynx and larynx. *J Surg Oncol* 6:357, 1974
4. Jesse RH, Fletcher GH: Metastases in cervical lymph nodes from oropharyngeal carcinoma; treatment and results. *Am J Surg* 112:547, 1966
5. Pollack RS: *Tumor Surgery of the Head and Neck,* pp 5, 15, 19, 90. Basel: Karger, 1975
6. Pollack RS: The diagnosis and treatment of head and neck cancer. *Oncology* 21:29, 1967
7. Abramson M, Schilling RW, Huang C, et al: Collagenase activity in epidermoid carcinoma of the oral cavity and larynx. *Ann Otol Rhinol Laryngol* 84:158, 1975
8. Eilber FR, Morton DL, Ketcham AS: Immunologic abnormalities in head and neck cancer. *Am J Surg* 128:534, 1974
9. Krull EA, Fellman AC, Fabian LA: White lesions of the mouth. *Clin Symp* 25:2, 1973
10. Whicker JH, DeSanto LW, Devine KD: Surgical treatment of squamous cell carcinoma of the tonsil. *Laryngoscope* 84:90, 1974
11. MacComb WS: Diagnosis and treatment of metastatic cervical cancerous nodes from an unknown primary site. *Am J Surg* 124:441, 1972

9

Parapharyngeal and retromandibular parotid tumor

A 35-year-old man was referred by an otorhinolaryngologist to a general surgeon with a subspecialty in head and neck surgery. The patient had been complaining of vague discomfort and an aching sensation on the right side of his throat. He was mildly diabetic but otherwise in good health.

On examination the only pertinent finding was a bulge in the right lateral pharyngeal wall. The so-called parapharyngeal swelling occupied the right posterolateral region of the pharynx, just distal to the tonsillar fossa. A tonsillectomy had been performed many years before. There was no evidence of any inflammation or pharyngitis. There were no enlarged lymph nodes in the neck. Chest and mandible X-rays were negative. A diagnosis of probable retromandibular and/or parapharyngeal tumor of the true deep lobe of the right parotid gland was made.

Surgical exploration of the right parotid gland and right parapharyngeal space was performed. The facial nerve was identified intact with all its branches and was not traumatized. The parotid gland appeared larger than normal, and the inferior half was described as swollen. This swelling seemed to be even more marked as the retromandibular and parapharyngeal space was exposed. It was presumed that the tumor was present within the lower half of the parotid gland. The inferior two-thirds of the lateral or superficial lobe of the parotid gland and all of the true deep lobe within the retromandibular space were removed. The facial nerve and its branches remained intact. The specimen was examined, but no tumor was found. Palpation of the parapharyngeal wall and musculature revealed a uniform, soft, diffuse enlargement with no identifiable neoplasm. The vagus nerve and internal carotid artery were explored superiorly and were normal without evidence of tumor. Nothing further was done.

Postoperative convalescence was unremarkable, but the right lateral pharyngeal wall bulge persisted and symptoms were unchanged. Six months later, Frey's syndrome (gustatory sweating), described as severe[1,2] developed. Severing Jacobson's nerve gave only temporary relief.[3,4] The patient again complained of throat discomfort.

A second surgeon re-explored the parapharyngeal recess through both an internal (oropharyngeal) and an external (neck) approach. A nondescript mass of xanthomatous, fibrous tissue was removed from a region more directly posterior than the usual posterolateral parapharyngeal space. Postoperatively the right lateral pharyngeal wall bulge was markedly reduced and symptoms abated. Suit was filed against the first surgeon, alleging incompetent and unnecessary surgery with failure to diagnose and/or remove a tumor and causing postoperative sequelae.

Discussion and comment. In the absence of an obvious surface or mucosal lesion, tonsillar abscess, or tumor, there are only a few neoplasms that cause a parapharyngeal or lateral pharyngeal wall bulge.[1,5-7] The most common are tumors of the true deep lobe of the parotid gland, tumors of the carotid body, tumors arising in the vagus nerve trunk as it courses through the parapharyngeal recess, and tumors arising in the ganglion nodosum of the vagus nerve. Theoretically, a tumor of the superior sympathetic ganglion may cause a lateral pharyngeal wall bulge, but this would be extremely rare since the tumor's location would be more posterior than lateral with regard to the pharynx. This anatomic structure should be avoided, if possible, during surgery for tumors situated at the more posterior-medial margin of the parapharyngeal recess.[1,5]

Anatomically there is a well-defined, open space just lateral to the pharyngeal wall.[5,6,8,9] It's bounded medially by the fascia of the pharynx itself, laterally by the pterygoid muscles and sheath of the parotid gland, above by the base of the skull and below by the attachment of the cervical fascia to the hyoid bone, submandibular gland, and mandible. Anteriorly, it becomes continuous with the submandibular space and extends to the pterygomandibular raphe and the spaces associated with the floor of the mouth. The posterior wall is formed by the connective tissue about the internal jugular vein and internal carotid artery, and extends beyond to the retropharyngeal space behind the pharynx.

The lateral parapharyngeal space is crowded with anatomic structures.[8,9] Running along the outer surface of the lateral pharyngeal wall of the pharynx, and in close relationship posterolaterally, are the 9th, 10th, and 11th cranial nerves as they emerge through the jugular foramen. The hypoglossal nerve crosses behind the structures coming from the jugular foramen, which include the internal jugular vein, and runs downward, laterally and forward. Anteromedial to all these is the internal carotid artery. Just lateral or external to all of them, and snuggled against the inner or medial table of the ascending ramus of the mandible, is the true deep, or retromandibular, lobe of the parotid gland.[1]

In this patient the presumptive diagnosis of a true-deep-lobe parotid gland was reasonable. Unfortunately, the rare, unexpected, and occult presence of a mass of nondescript tissue deep in the parapharyngeal recess compounded the diagnostic and therapeutic dilemma. A thorough exploration of the lateral parapharyngeal space could well necessitate parotid gland resection with dissection and preservation of the seventh nerve to rule out the presence of a tumor either in that gland or in the space itself. In turn, removing part or all of the parotid facilitates examination of the vagus nerve and the region about the carotid body. In the second operation the mass of nondescript tissue causing the patient's signs and symptoms was reached and removed, but this time resection was made easier by the exploration and removal of parotid tissue performed at the first operation. Such are the intricacies of surgery in complex anatomic areas, and the dependence of one surgeon on another. Nevertheless, the first surgeon was exposed to allegations of incompetence, no matter how questionable the charge.

Frey's syndrome is seen in about 60 per cent of patients who undergo resection of the major portion of the lateral or superficial parotid lobe.[1-4] It was this factor that led the patient to charge malpractice. Symptoms caused by Frey's syndrome will regress spontaneously with time. Perhaps that's why efforts to minimize the sweating phenomenon with a Jacobson's or tympanic neurectomy have met with varying degrees of success.[3,4,10]

The patient in this case sued the doctor despite the lack of serious sequelae or real damage. Here's an excellent example of a gap between the patient's expectation of results and the complexities and difficulties the surgeon encounters in striving for those results. All too often, unrealistic expectations lie behind the allegations made against the physician. The complexity of the problem and the expertise involved seem to matter very little.

References

1. Pollack RS: *Tumor Surgery of the Head and Neck*, p 134. Basel: Karger, 1975
2. Spiro RH, Martin HE: Gustatory sweating following parotid surgery and radical neck dissection. *Ann Surg* 165:118, 1965

3. Hunt W, Joseph D, Newell R, et al: Gustatory sweating. *Arch Otolaryngol* 83:260, 1966
4. Smith RO, Hemenway WG, Stevens KM, et al: Jacobson's neurectomy for Frey's syndrome. *Am J Surg* 120:478, 1970
5. Patey DH, Thackray AC: Pathological anatomy and treatment of parotid tumours with retropharyngeal extension (dumb-bell tumours). *Br J Surg* 44:352, 1956-1957
6. Pollack RS: Retromandibular and parapharyngeal tumors: Diagnostic and therapeutic dilemma. *Proc 46th Gen Sci Meet Roy Australasian Coll Surg (Singapore),* p 712. Singapore: Eurasia Press, 1973
7. Work WP, Gates GA: Tumors of the parotid gland and parapharyngeal space. *Otolaryngol Clin North Am* 2:497, 1969
8. Hollinshead WH: *Anatomy for Surgeons,* 2nd ed, vol 1, pp 321-323, Figs. 5-15, 5-18. New York: Hoeber Medical Division, Harper & Row, 1968
9. Hollinshead WH: *Anatomy for Surgeons,* 2nd ed, vol 1, pp 455, 527. New York: Hoeber Medical Division, Harper & Row, 1968
10. Hemenway WG: Gustatory sweating and flushing. *Laryngoscope* 70:84, 1960

10

Post-thyroidectomy bilateral vocal cord paralysis

A 38-year-old woman, after adequate preoperative preparation with antithyroid medication, was operated upon for a large, toxic goiter. A near-total thyroidectomy was performed, leaving only an estimated 2 gm of thyroid on the right side lying against the trachea. Immediately after the operation, the patient was hoarse and had difficulty in breathing, but these symptoms gradually improved over the next 48 hours and never reached emergency proportions. She improved further and was discharged on the sixth postoperative day, still hoarse and breathing with a little difficulty and some stridor.

Over the next 10 months dyspnea continued, especially on exertion, and hoarseness did not improve much although the patient's voice became slightly stronger. Examination of her vocal cords during the first few months postoperatively was said to show mobility of the cords, but they did not meet in the midline. By the sixth month after surgery, the cords were described as showing some motion but did not close. At 10 months postoperatively, the cords were described as being very close together but able to move. Laryngeal stridor and exertional dyspnea grew worse. One year after thyroidectomy, a laryngologist described the condition as bilateral abduction vocal cord paralysis.

Dyspnea and shortness of breath increased still further. A right arytenoidectomy with temporary tracheostomy was performed 17 months following thyroid surgery. The patient obtained relief in breathing to an estimated normal degree, but her voice remained an airy whisper. Thyrotoxicity did not recur. Suit was filed, claiming loss of voice due to incompetent surgery.

Discussion and comment. Large thyroid glands, toxic or nontoxic, benign or malignant, can be extremely difficult technical problems for the surgeon. The vulnerability of the recurrent (inferior) laryngeal nerves is readily apparent.[1,2] To divide or injure one of these nerves inadvertently in a difficult case of benign thyroid disease may be considered excusable or acceptable and a calculated risk of indicated surgery. And damage to one nerve and resulting vocal cord paralysis can be overcome simply and with good voice recovery by injecting the tissue immediately lateral to the cord with Teflon or silicone, which pushes the cord to a fixed position at the midline. This makes the opposite, nonparalyzed cord approximate at the midline, and the voice becomes greatly improved. Furthermore, breathing is rarely compromised with paralysis of one cord, since the glottic space remains open wide enough for the passage of air.

Even though paralysis of one vocal cord is acceptable, especially in a patient with a difficult thyroid problem,[2] liability is still a real consideration. Not only do patients expect modern surgery to produce perfect results, but toxic thyroid disease can often be treated with radioiodine instead of surgery. Before undertaking a predictably difficult toxic goiter operation, surgeon and patient should discuss the radioiodine alternative.

When both cords are paralyzed, the damage is obviously compounded and the surgeon's exposure becomes acute.[3] Life-endangering respiratory distress can occur. Relief demands not only tracheostomy as a temporary expedient but arytenoidectomy as a permanent one, which reduces the patient's voice to a hoarse whisper.

When the vocal cords are paralyzed by recurrent nerve injury, as a rule they'll assume partial abduction from the midline for three to six months. Immediately following nerve injury, the cords are abducted in a relatively limp state. Therefore, the motion of the extrinsic laryngeal muscles, mediated through the superior laryngeal nerve, will actually move the vocal cords and give a false impression of a functioning recurrent (inferior) nerve.[1] In this limp phase, vigorous inhaling or exhaling may cause the cords to flutter, which is also misleading. Nonetheless, the cords will not move toward the midline on phonation and certainly will not approximate. The voice is hoarse and weak, but variably so. As time passes, the cords become stiffened through atrophy. This stiffening process draws the cords closer to the midline, so that the voice actually improves. Phonation is aided by the intrinsic laryngeal muscles, which tend to draw the cords closer, since the adductors are stronger than the abductors.

The abduction position keeps enough glottic space open to permit adequate or barely adequate breathing. With the passage of time, however, the cords move slowly, almost imperceptibly, toward the midline, further narrowing the glottis. Ultimately no glottic space remains. This process may be hastened by infection, inflammation, or a foreign body. The situation becomes truly life-endangering.

In the patient under study, it was indeed fortunate—and unusual—that an emergency didn't arise. Luckily the cords became fixed in abduction, and movement toward the midline was slow without approximation, thus allowing for some airway, however insecure.

The surgeon's liability and exposure are due not so much to a technical error resulting in cord paralysis but to not acting quickly to alleviate a life-endangering situation. To delay on the mistaken assumption that the paralysis is temporary or because of erroneous interpretation of cord motion, which is probably secondary to breathing, does not appear reasonable. With no return of motion after three months, certainly six, cord paralysis should be considered permanent.

References

1. *Morris' Human Anatomy,* 9th ed, p 1322. Philadelphia: Blakiston, 1933
2. Pollack RS: *Tumor Surgery of the Head and Neck,* pp 149-163. Basel: Karger, 1975
3. Perzik SL: *Surgery in Thyroid Disease,* p 200. New York: Stratton, 1976

11

Nonrecurrent laryngeal nerve

A 36-year-old man complaining of a lump on his neck was seen by a board-certified general surgeon. The lump had been present for about two months and was situated in the midportion of the right side of the neck, in front of the sternocleidomastoid muscle. It was silent. Thorough head and neck examination was unremarkable. A chest X-ray was reported to be normal, and there were no other signs or symptoms of disease.

A presumptive diagnosis of cervical lymph node lymphoma was made. At operation, a transverse incision was made in the skin of the right neck overlying the tumor. The latter was situated at about the level of the cricothyroid articulation, perhaps slightly below the level of the cricoid cartilage. Deeper dissection revealed a discrete tumor, freely movable, 3 by 4 cm, situated on the lateral aspect of the upper and midportion of the thyroid gland. It was resected completely, along with the upper pole and midportion of the right lobe of the thyroid gland, to which it was lightly attached. The lower half of the right thyroid lobe was left in place and not rotated out of its bed. During dissection and removal, the superior half of the right thyroid was lifted out of its fossa and turned medially, but dissection did not go below this point; i.e., structures behind the inferior portion of the gland were not exposed.

The tumor proved to be a benign adenoma of thyroid origin. The postoperative course was marked by hoarseness with some difficulty in swallowing and with aspiration of food and saliva. Swallowing returned to normal within a few days but the hoarseness persisted. Indirect laryngoscopy revealed a paralyzed right vocal cord.

It did not recover. Six months later, a Teflon injection behind and lateral to the paralyzed cord moved it to the midline of the glottic space, thus allowing for approximation of the mobile, functioning opposite cord and giving a much improved voice. Suit was filed, claiming that inadequate preoperative studies and incompetent surgery resulted in hoarseness.

Discussion and comment. When the average adult with a lump on the side of the upper neck is examined, the most likely diagnosis is that the lump is a metastasis within a lymph node from a primary cancer in the oral cavity, oropharynx, or larynx. The primary sites of cancer in these anatomic areas can be occult and remain hidden for months.

If a complete history is taken and careful examination of the head and neck reveals no obvious primary cancer, and if a thorough X-ray study of the chest, perhaps including isotope scans, is negative, the wisest course to pursue next is biopsy (excisional if feasible) of the neck tumor.

Much has been written concerning a solitary lymph node metastasis in the neck and an esoteric primary cancer.[1,2] It's outside the scope of this case review to discuss that subject further, but it should be at least mentioned in terms of the patient's allegations of inadequate preoperative study. After thorough examination and chest X-rays, excisional biopsy is indicated and may itself be considered further study. So-called blind biopsy of the hypopharynx or nasopharynx, especially if the metastases are of the squamous cell type, would come after that.

It's debatable whether blind biopsies of these esoteric areas to find the exact source of the primary cancer should take precedence over neck tumor biopsy. In actual practice, it's better to biopsy the neck lymph node metastasis first. The primary cancer may not be detectable for many months despite multiple blind biopsies, the cancer may have started in an area below the clavicle, or the neck tumor could represent an incipient form of lymphoma. Definitive treatment, curative or palliative, can then be started without delay, and an earlier, more complete understanding is obtained of the clinical and histologic problem. In this patient, once tumor excision was performed, there obviously was no need for added investigative procedures since the possibility of lymphoma was ruled out. The allegations of inadequate preoperative study therefore appear to be without merit.

In Chapter 10, injury to the recurrent laryngeal nerve during thyroid surgery was discussed in full. With the location of the tumor in the right side of this patient's neck, and considering the technique used, it's difficult to see how the recurrent laryngeal nerve was damaged. With a tumor actually situated lateral to the superior and midportion of the right thyroid gland (aberrant thyroid?), removal of only the upper half of the gland would suggest that the surgery was performed in an area well removed from the usual course of the recurrent laryngeal nerve.[3] This would be so unless dissection was extended to the area of the crico-tracheo-esophageal junction, where the nerve and its branches dip into the laryngeal structures.[2,4] But apparently dissection was simple and easily performed in this patient, since the tumor was mobile and only slightly attached to the right side of the thyroid gland at its upper and midportion.

It's well known that isolating, ligating, and dividing the superior thyroid vessels make the external branch of the superior laryngeal nerve vulnerable to inadvertent damage.[4,5] That's good reason to ligate the superior pole vessels individually, not as a mass bundle.[2,3] In this patient that particular nerve branch may have been traumatized, but it's impossible to be certain in view of the accompanying vocal cord paralysis. The transient difficulties with aspiration and swallowing experienced postoperatively are suggestive. These symptoms will also follow trauma to the superior laryngeal nerve itself and/or its internal branch as well.

The external branch of the superior laryngeal nerve is close to the superior thyroid artery in 85 per cent of cadaver dissections.[5,6] My own experience suggests an even higher percentage. Difficult surgical dissection at the superior thyroid pole naturally will enhance the likelihood of trauma to this nerve. Ligatures about the superior pole vessels should be carefully and individually placed. The external branch of the superior laryngeal nerve contains motor fibers to the cricothyroid muscle. This muscle maintains the tone of the true vocal cord.[3,5,6] Motion of the cord is not impaired when this nerve is traumatized, but with prolonged use or under stress the cord loses its tone and timbre. As Harrison[5] noted, it becomes "tired" and less resonant. Although the consequences of damage to this nerve are not as drastic as damage to the recurrent laryngeal nerve, its function is nonetheless important. This is especially so in patients who are dependent on the quality of their voice for a livelihood.

In view of the location of the tumor and the area dissected in this patient, how can one best explain the cord paralysis? It's very likely that paralysis of the right vocal cord occurred from inadvertent cutting of a nonrecurrent laryngeal nerve. In approximately 1 per cent of patients (fewer in my experience) the nerve to the vocal cord will arise directly from the vagus on the right side. It is said to be due to an anomalous origin of the right subclavian artery from a persistent sixth aortic arch.[5] The nonrecurrent laryngeal nerve, as described well by Perzik,[4] usually emerges from beneath the carotid-vagus complex at or below the level of the lower border of the cricoid cartilage. It courses directly in a brief, transverse, medial manner and then upward to the crico-tracheo-esophageal junction. It may often leave the vagus at a lower level, the third or fourth tracheal ring. Except in a patient with situs inversus, a nonrecurrent laryngeal nerve will be present only on the right side.

The surgery performed on this patient was in the area traversed by a nonrecurrent laryngeal nerve that emerged from the vagus at the cricoid level and thus was vulnerable to inadvertent damage. It would reasonably explain how such a complication could occur when surgery was performed in an area well removed from the usual, expected course of a nonanomalous recurrent nerve.

Teflon injection behind and lateral to the paralyzed cord resulted in marked improvement of the voice and permitted adequate glottic space for respiration. The damage to the patient was therefore much lessened. This complication would appear acceptable (see Chapter 10) and made more so by a rare anatomic anomaly.

References

1. MacComb WS: Diagnosis and treatment of metastatic cervical cancerous nodes from an unknown primary site. *Am J Surg* 124:441, 1972
2. Pollack RS: *Tumor Surgery of the Head and Neck*, pp 6, 13, 158. Basel: Karger, 1975
3. *Morris' Human Anatomy*, 9th ed, p 1322. Philadelphia: Blakiston, 1933
4. Perzik SL: *Surgery in Thyroid Disease*, p 96. New York: Stratton, 1976
5. Harrison TS: The non-recurrent laryngeal nerve. In *Davis-Christopher Textbook of Surgery (Sabiston DC, ed)*, 11th ed, p 688. Philadelphia: Saunders, 1977
6. Durham CF, Harrison TS: The surgical anatomy of the superior laryngeal nerve. *Surg Gynecol Obstet* 118:38, 1964

12

Thyroiditis and thyroid cancer

A 10-year-old boy complaining of an enlarged thyroid gland was seen by a board-certified surgeon. He was in otherwise good general health and was developing normally. The enlargement was essentially silent, although some slight pain and tenderness were described. There were no pressure symptoms and no other pertinent history.

On examination the patient was found to be a healthy, normal-appearing, thin child in no distress. Physical findings were limited to the thyroid gland, which was estimated to be three times larger than normal, diffusely and evenly so. There was very slight tenderness to palpation, but no redness of the overlying skin. The gland felt firm, rubbery, and diffusely lobulated, more so on the left. In the midportion of this lobe there was the suggestion of a nodule. There were no enlarged lymph nodes in the neck and no signs or symptoms of clinical hyperthyroidism. A diagnosis of thyroiditis (Hashimoto's, lymphocytic, struma lymphomatosa) was made. Routine laboratory studies, complete blood count, and urinalysis were within normal limits, but the erythrocyte sedimentation rate was very slightly elevated. A chest X-ray was unremarkable. Specific films of the thyroid area were not taken.

A radioactive scan with $[^{7,5}\mathrm{Se}]$selenomethionine was interpreted to show the spotty uptake characteristic of thyroiditis. Serum protein-bound iodine was very slightly elevated, but serum thyroxine and triiodothyronine were normal. Radioimmunoassay studies to demonstrate circulating antibodies reactive to thyroglobulins or to antigens from the thyroid epithelial cells were within normal limits. The diagnosis was felt to be thyroiditis nonetheless, and the patient was observed for six weeks. During this brief period there was little change in physical findings and the patient remained well.

Over the next three months the entire gland became more firm, lobulated, and nodular, especially on the left, with little reduction in overall size. The nodule in the left lobe appeared more distinct. Desiccated thyroid extract, 3 gr daily, was prescribed, but after 10 weeks of this medication the gland showed no change. In fact, the left lobe was described as seeming larger, as was the nodule mentioned above, and now another nodule was felt in the right lobe. Both left and right lobe nodules were hard and firm.

The patient was kept on suppressive thyroid therapy as before. A repeat serum antibody titer test was done and this time was reported to be positive, supporting the diagnosis of thyroiditis. A follow-up examination two months later, now almost nine months following the initial visit, revealed two firmly enlarged lymph nodes in the left neck anterior to the sternomastoid muscle and just below the level of the carotid bulb.[1] Excisional biopsy revealed papillary adenocarcinoma consistent with thyroid origin.

A total thyroidectomy was subsequently performed. It revealed papillary adenocarcinoma in both lobes. Two months later, modified neck dissections performed first on the left and then on the right side showed multiple cervical lymph node metastases.

The patient continued to receive suppressive thyroid medication postoperatively. Despite this, on two separate occasions over the ensuing year additional cervical lymph node metastases developed, one on each side of the neck, requiring further surgical excision (berry picking).

A radioiodine isotope scan taken eight months after the last neck node surgical excision was negative for any uptake in the neck or mediastinum. The lungs remained clear on X-rays throughout the patient's entire course. He was alive and well without recurrent cancer four years following thyroidectomy.

Suit was filed, alleging delay in the diagnosis of thyroid cancer leading to diminished chances of cure and necessitating additional neck surgery.

Discussion and comment. The occurrence of thyroid cancer in persons between 10 and 20 years of age following irradiation exposure to the thyroid during their earlier years is, of course, well established.[2-5] The increased incidence of thyroid cancer in patients with lymphocytic thyroiditis (Hashimoto's, struma lymphomatosa), however, is only just being recognized.

The term thyroiditis itself can be misleading. Acute bacterial thyroiditis, often of streptococcal origin in the pharynx and seen with some frequency in years past, is a disappearing disease but still occurs despite our era of antibiotic exuberance. When it's associated with formation of a thyroid abscess, surgical drainage is necessary.

Another form of thyroiditis, de Quervain's, sometimes called granulomatous thyroiditis or subacute thyroiditis, is a disease of moderately abrupt onset and, like acute thyroiditis, may follow a respiratory infection.[6,7] The thyroid becomes enlarged, full, congested (but not firmly so), and tender. Repeated remissions and exacerbations of the disease may continue for several months. Antibiotics, although useful, are not necessarily curative. The disease process seems to be self-limiting in most cases. The white blood count is usually normal or even depressed (suggesting a viral etiology?), but the erythrocyte sedimentation rate is elevated. Thyroid function in most patients is not disturbed, although thyrotoxicosis has been reported during the illness itself.[8] As a rule, the thyroid regains its normal activity after recovery.

The condition at issue here is best termed lymphocytic thyroiditis, first described by Hashimoto in 1912. In the experience of myself and others,[6-8] it's definitely on the rise, though admittedly better recognition may account for the increased incidence.

The thyroid gland presents very much as described in this patient. In the initial stages of the disease, mild hyperthyroidism may be present as the result of release of stored hormone.[6,8] It clears rapidly. The most frequent clinical findings, especially as seen by the surgeon, are mild hypothyroidism and a thyroid gland that is slightly enlarged throughout, lobulated, firm, even granular in places, nontender, and with one or more localized nodules in one or both lobes. Pressure symptoms or vague discomfort on swallowing or when lying down are not infrequent. I've found thyroid scans to be only moderately helpful in differentiating this disease from cancer.[9] Most surgeons, when confronted with this clinical picture, are forced into open biopsy and exploration[3,6,10] Thorough evaluation at operation is obviously the sine qua non of good surgery. Once the diagnosis is assured, pressure symptoms, if present because of tracheal constriction, can be simply relieved by dividing or removing the thyroid isthmus.

Some patients with lymphocytic thyroiditis will have circulating antibodies reactive to either thyroglobulin or antigens from their own thyroid epithelial cells, the so-called autoimmune mechanism. A diagnostic antibody titer may not always be present, however, and results of the test, which is most accurate when done by radioimmunoassay, can be capricious.

The characteristic microscopic picture of this disease is one of lymphocytic infiltration. Eventual recovery of normal thyroid function depends on the degree of infiltration with its attendant obliteration of the thyroid acini. Obliteration of acini could well be related to the duration of the disease. As a rule, the majority of patients will require exogenous thyroid hormone to combat hypothyroidism.

Concomitant with the recognized increase in thyroiditis in adults has been the realization that it occurs in children too, although probably less often. Since the incidence of papillary adenocarcinoma of the thyroid is increased in adult patients with chronic thyroiditis, it must be assumed that a similar situation exists with children and adolescents. It follows, therefore, that even when there's no history of prior radiation in a child in whom thyroiditis has been diagnosed, cancer can be an unwelcome accompaniment or sequela.

The degree to which cancer of this histologic type is actually lethal in children has been the subject of much debate,[5, 11] I've observed children and adolescents with papillary adenocarcinoma of the thyroid for many years and have yet to see it as a specific cause of death. Undoubtedly it can be fatal, but the biology of this form of cancer in young individuals seems unpredictable and puzzling.

To differentiate between lymphocytic thyroiditis and cancer of the thyroid in a 10-year-old boy is a challenge that requires the utmost diagnostic acumen. The difficulty confronting the surgeon is clearly illustrated with this patient. Nonetheless, the association between the two conditions is recognized, and the indication for surgical exploration of a nodule in the thyroid of a child, if it doesn't quickly respond to exogenous thyroid, is absolute.[3, 10] A nodule appearing in a euthyroid child has at least a 50 per cent chance (probably greater in my experience) of being cancer.[6]

References

1. Pollack RS: Cervical lymph node metastasis of thyroid cancer. *Am J Surg* 102:388, 1961
2. Foster RS: Thyroid irradiation and carcinogenesis. *Am J Surg* 130:608, 1975
3. Perzik SL: *Surgery in Thyroid Disease,* p 227. New York: Stratton, 1976
4. Refetoff S, Harrison JH, Karanfilski BT, et al: Continuing occurrence of thyroid carcinoma after irradiation to the neck in infancy and childhood. *N Engl J Med* 292:171, 1975
5. Winship T, Roxvall RV: Thyroid carcinoma in childhood: Final report on a twenty year study. *Clin Proc Child Hosp* 26:11, 1970
6. Harrison TS: Thyroiditis. In *Davis-Christopher Textbook of Surgery* (Sabiston DC, ed), 11th ed, pp 690, 703, 706, 707. Philadelphia: Saunders, 1977
7. Personal communications
8. Gluck FB, Nusynowitz ML, Plymate S: Chronic lymphocytic thyroiditis, thyrotoxicosis and low radioactive iodine uptake. *N Engl J Med* 293:624, 1975
9. Thomas CG Jr, Pepper FD, Owen J: Differentiation of malignant from benign lesions of the thyroid gland using complementary scanning with 75-selenomethionine and radioiodide. *Ann Surg* 170:396, 1969
10. Pollack RS: *Tumor Surgery of the Head and Neck,* p 150. Basel: Karger, 1975
11. Buckwalter JA, Thomas CG Jr, Freeman JB: Is childhood thyroid cancer a lethal disease? *Ann Surg* 181:632, 1975

13

The breast

Malpractice cases involving the breast are increasing, yet should be relatively easy to avoid. Whether this can be done successfully depends on one's knowledge of the major risks involved.

Failure to diagnose cancer of the breast. This charge is a potential hazard for any physician who examines women. To minimize the risk, (1) make certain your examination includes a thorough check for breast cancer; (2) record your findings on your office chart or on the patient's hospital record; a simple diagram is very supportive; (3) if you suspect cancer, insist that the patient have a further investigation, i.e., biopsy or close re-examination, and note on her chart that you recommended it; (4) consider mammograms and consultation.

An Eastern surgeon spent many hours with his attorneys over a patient who had been referred to him for a cholecystectomy. He did an office examination about a week before he had the woman admitted to the hospital. The surgery went smoothly, and the patient was full of praise for her doctor. He was very much startled several months later to find himself named in a malpractice suit as a codefendant with the referring internist. Both doctors were charged with careless failure to detect and treat carcinoma of the breast. The patient was demanding a large figure in damages.

Another doctor had later detected the cancer and had done a radical mastectomy. Although the patient's attorney could prove a missed diagnosis, he couldn't show how much harm his client had suffered because of the few months' delay in getting the cancer treated. He finally dropped the case against the surgeon entirely and settled for a minor "nuisance" sum from the internist's insurance carrier.

Injury or death following radiotherapy for breast cancer. Physicians who practice radiotherapy still pay one of the highest premium rates for malpractice insurance. Yet such a physician won't find the premiums extravagant if he's ever handed a complaint charging him with $3 million worth of malpractice damages.

The most frequent malpractice charge in radiation therapy is overdosage, and the first thing a plaintiff's attorney will look for is a malfunctioning machine. If you perform X-ray therapy, make certain the machine is calibrated regularly. The frequency of calibration will depend on your own judgment and experience as well as on the manufacturer's instructions. It's best to be ultraconservative. If you have a full- or part-time physicist with you, keep in close consultation with him. This will strengthen your position.

One case in point involved a roentgenologist and a patient who was referred to him for radiation therapy following a left radical mastectomy. After two weeks of treatment, she complained of a burning sensation over the incision. The doctor prescribed a salve and continued the X-ray treatments for another two months, although the patient's left side turned red and began to weep and fissure. Shortly afterward, some tissue in the irradiated field, more than 15 cm in diameter, sloughed from her chest wall, exposing the ribs. She hemorrhaged, went into shock, and died. Her daughter brought suit for several million dollars. A settlement followed almost before the ink had dried on the complaint.

The plaintiff's attorney won his case in three pretrial maneuvers, standard tactics in radiation overdosage suits. First, he got a court order permitting him to have an expert examine the physician's X-ray machine. The examination showed that the machine was delivering an excess dosage. Second, the lawyer subpoenaed the company that serviced the machine. He learned that no one had checked the machine for more than six months, even though the manufacturer had recommended calibration every three months. Third, at the examination before trial, the lawyer forced the roentgenologist to admit he hadn't had anyone else calibrate his machine during those six months.

A trial was out of the question. Since the machine's error had been so clearly shown, even the defendant would have been hard pressed to justify the dosage. The settlement figure was high.

The story isn't too different when cobalt or a linear accelerator is used as the source of radiation. Even when given in proper dosage, radioactive cobalt will damage healthy tissue. The courts, knowing this, will not hold you responsible for any damage provided you can prove that you explained the risk to your patient and received her informed consent.

To protect yourself legally, therefore, take two steps prior to giving cobalt or accelerator treatment: (1) Tell the patient, preferably before a witness, exactly what radioactive cobalt can do to her if the therapy goes awry, and (2) have the patient sign a realistic consent form that specifically spells out the dangers you've discussed with her. Unless you've taken both precautions, your chances of winning a jury to your side in case of a suit are slim. A Louisiana roentgenologist found this out.

His patient, who had suffered severe radiation sickness, swore that she would never have consented to the treatment if the full risk had been explained to her. The defendant doctor claimed that he had explained the risk. The trouble was that he had no witnesses to back him up, and his patient had signed only a blanket consent form allowing him to do whatever his judgment dictated. The jury awarded her a sizable amount.

That award was less than one a New York physician had to pay. The situation was identical except that the patient, a 40-year-old mother of two children, died. The doctor's lawyer settled.

Mammoplasty mishaps and claims of poor results. Legally, this type of cosmetic/reconstructive surgery poses a greater risk than any other medical procedure except electroshock therapy. Maximum malpractice coverage is essential because the proportion of patients who are dissatisfied with the results of a mammoplasty is high. With changing opinions regarding the surgical treatment of breast cancer and related precancerous lesions, breast reconstruction with an implant is frequently performed. These patients tend to sue whether they have legal grounds or not.

One surgeon did a mammoplasty on a self-styled "entertainer." Unhappy about the results, she's been hauling him through the courts ever since. When the attorneys for his insurance company get the case dismissed periodically, she simply hires another lawyer and starts the suit again in another court. She can't prove her case, and it probably will never get to trial. But until she gives up or dies, the surgeon needs about $1,500 to $3,000 worth of legal services a year. Fortunately, his malpractice insurance covers him for cosmetic surgery, so he doesn't pay those defense costs out of his own pocket.

Sometimes the tables are turned and it's the defense that doesn't have a leg to stand on. A surgeon who was sued for causing the loss of a nipple following a mammoplasty "couldn't imagine how it happened." The plaintiff's attorney could. He told the defense counsel that the surgeon rotated the areola in such a way as to compromise the blood vessels leading to the nipple and cause atrophy. "Read the hospital record and send me a check."

He got a large one. Afterward, the plaintiff's lawyer remarked: "Surgeons should realize that what they do isn't a secret anymore. Any good lawyer can find out enough about an operation to tell a jury what went wrong."

That's a comment worth remembering. Performing a mammoplasty or any breast surgery without the proper training and skill is an opening invitation for some plaintiff's lawyer to "tell a jury what went wrong."

Although a surgeon can't usually tell beforehand whether a patient will be satisfied with the results of a mammoplasty, he can take steps to ward off the legal tangles that result when she is dissatisfied. He can explain to the patient the nature, risks, and complexities of the operation in the presence of one or, preferably, two witnesses. She must understand that he is making no guarantee or promise of a particular result. He should then have the patient sign a detailed consent form stating exactly that.

Under no circumstances should a surgeon show his patient any photographs, models, statuary, or similar illustrations of a "perfect" breast. If he does, he may have a difficult time convincing a jury that he hadn't suggested the operation would produce a specific result.

14

Breast cancer: Diagnosis and mammography

A 43-year-old woman had painful breasts for over a year. On two occasions during this period she was examined by her physician, a board-certified obstetrician-gynecologist. There was no evidence of anything significant in her breasts that would suggest cancer. The physician didn't order mammograms since he felt that clinical examination didn't warrant them. The patient, although reassured, still had painful breasts and thought that she herself felt a lump in the upper outer quadrant of the right breast. Eight months after her last examination, another doctor found a tumor in the upper outer quadrant of the right breast. Biopsy proved it malignant, and a modified radical mastectomy was performed; 2 out of a total of 16 lymph nodes situated in the lower axilla contained metastases. The tumor was negative for estrogen receptor protein. The patient received chemotherapy. At the time her case was reviewed, she had been alive and well without recurrence for over two years. But suit was filed, alleging delay in the diagnosis of cancer and failure to perform mammography.

Discussion and comment. Delay in the diagnosis of breast cancer is alleged too often and too easily. The actual effect of delay on prognosis has been well covered in Chapters 2 and 46. There's growing appreciation of the roles of cellular biology and the tumor-host relationship, which to a reasonable extent mitigate the effect of delay and, therefore, the charge of malpractice.

The publication of numerous reports on mammography[1-6] and its general acceptance by the laity have created additional exposure for the physician who doesn't always utilize this modality but nevertheless does his utmost to diagnose breast cancer without undue delay. Despite initial enthusiastic reports regarding mammography, it has limitations and cannot be considered wholly innocuous.[7-10]

Mammography is not infallible. Errors in interpretation are

especially prevalent among women under 35, an age group where cancer diagnosis is most difficult. Although the degree of hazardous radiation exposure is being debated, it certainly exists.[11-14]

The chief value of mammography is purported to lie in the detection of early or what is now termed minimal breast cancer.[15-17] The report of Strax et al[6] seems to substantiate this by citing improved survival rates in women who received mammography. Yet a word of caution must be interjected: Even "minimal" breast cancers may already be disseminated when detected by mammography and thus are actually not early, but late.[15, 18] As Ackerman and Katzenstein have noted,[15] the growth rate of the primary cancer seems to have little influence on the probability of metastatic dissemination. Iliac crest biopsies are positive in some patients with so-called early cancers and negative bone scans. It seems apparent, therefore, that many "early, localized" breast cancers have long since metastasized.

It is very likely that cure of breast cancer depends on the body's ability to destroy, through an immune mechanism, those cancer cells which have already spread from the primary site of tumor formation. All too many experienced clinicians can recall patients with primary breast cancers 1 cm in size or even less and situated in the upper outer quadrant, and with negative axillary lymph nodes, who developed disseminated metastases to the spine, lungs, and liver three, four, or even eight years after mastectomy.

The discussion above in no way condones incompetence or procrastination.[8] It's an attempt to reveal the true natural history of a complicated biologic process that diagnostic and therapeutic efforts may influence very little.

In this patient, the value of mammography is wholly debatable. If judgment is to remain the province of the experienced clinician, certainly this must apply to the ordering or not ordering of X-rays. Unfortunately, it's all too often an issue in forensic medicine.

References

1. Bjurstam N, Hedberg K, Hultborn KA, et al: Diagnosis of breast carcinoma: Evaluation of clinical examination, mammography, thermography and aspiration biopsy. *Progr Surg* 13:1, 1974
2. Dodd GD: Present status of thermography, ultrasound and mammography in breast cancer detection. *Cancer* 39:2796, 1977
3. Egan RL: ***Mammography***, 2nd ed, pp 181, 184-186. Springfield, Ill: Thomas, 1972
4. Lesnick GJ: Detection of breast cancer in young women. *JAMA* 237:967, 1977
5. Rogers JV, Powell RW: Mammographic indications for biopsy of clinically normal breasts: Correlation with pathologic findings in 72 cases. *Am J Roentgenol Radium Ther Nucl Med* 115:794, 1972
6. Strax P, Venet L, Shapiro S: Value of mammography in reduction of mortality from breast cancer in mass screening. *Am J Roentgenol Radium Ther Nucl Med* 117:686, 1973
7. Egan RL: Mammography, radiation dose, and carcinogenicity. *Breast Dis Breast* 3(1):42, 1977
8. Egan RL: Breast biopsy priority. Cancer versus benign preoperative masses. *Cancer* 35:612, 1975

9. Simon N: Breast cancer induced by radiation. Relation to mammography and treatment of acne. *JAMA* 237:789, 1977
10. Swartz HM, Reichling BA: The risks of mammograms. *JAMA* 237:965, 1977
11. Boice JD Jr, Monson RR: Breast cancer in women after repeated fluoroscopic examinations of the chest. *J Natl Cancer Inst* 59:823, 1977
12. Editorial: Radiation-induced breast cancer. *Br Med J* 1(6055):191, 1977
13. Shore RE, Hempelmann LH, Kowaluk E, et al: Breast neoplasms in women treated with X-rays for acute postpartum mastitis. *J Natl Cancer Inst* 59:799, 1977
14. Simon N, Silverstone SM: Radiation as a cause of breast cancer. *Bull NY Acad Med* 52:741, 1976
15. Ackerman LV, Katzenstein AL: The concept of minimal breast cancer and the pathologist's role in the diagnosis of "early carcinoma." *Cancer* 39:2755, 1977
16. Rosen PP, Snyder RE, Robbins G: Specimen radiography for nonpalpable breast lesions found by mammography: Procedures and results. *Cancer* 35:1095, 1975
17. Rosen P, Snyder RE, Urban J, et al: Correlation of suspicious mammograms and X-rays of breast biopsies during surgery: Results in 60 cases. *Cancer* 31:656, 1973
18. Smith JA III, Gamez-Araujo JJ, Gallager HS, et al: Carcinoma of the breast: Analysis of total lymph node involvement versus level of metastasis. *Cancer* 39:527, 1977

15

Breast cancer: Mammograms and mastectomy

A 48-year-old woman consulted her family physician because of breast tenderness. Examination revealed what was termed fibrocystic disease of both breasts. Mammograms were not ordered. No definite appointment for re-examination was made. The patient had been prescribed an oral estrogen for several months, and this was continued. The dosage was said to be low. Because the breast tenderness continued, she saw another physician three months later. Left breast biopsy was performed in a central area just above the areola margin. It revealed multiple foci of infiltrating duct cancer. A modified radical mastectomy was performed; one axillary lymph node contained a metastasis. The patient received chemotherapy. Suit was filed against the family physician, claiming delay in the diagnosis of cancer, with the additional allegation that the delay made mastectomy necessary.

Discussion and comment. This case illustrates several vexing aspects of malpractice exposure. They culminate in the familiar charge of "therefore requiring extensive surgery"—in this case, mastectomy.

Mammography, a valuable procedure, though certainly not infallible, is an indicated adjunct for diagnosis in this patient's age group. Nonetheless, it must be coordinated with the clinical findings. Although it may be wise to obtain baseline mammograms in a 48-year-old patient whose clinical diagnosis is fibrocystic disease, the routine, indiscriminate use of ancillary laboratory tests and X-rays is open to criticism.[1-4]

Prescribing estrogens is another familiar target of malpractice suits related to breast cancer (see Chapter 16). At least at this juncture, there's doubt about the etiologic relationship between estrogens and breast cancer. I'm often amused at women who sit before me concernedly discussing the dangers of ingesting tiny amounts of estrogens, but who placidly smoke two packs of cigarettes a day. The fact that very small amounts of these hormones can make the difference between misery and comfort seems to be forgotten in the mania called cancerphobia.

Early diagnosis of breast cancer, in the hope of obviating the need for total mastectomy, is a worthy objective.[5-7] I don't know of any well-trained surgeon who enjoys performing a radical, modified, or simple mastectomy. Unfortunately, there's no other form of therapy that can be conscientiously recommended at this time.[8-11] Multiple sites of origin within the breast, micrometastases in axillary lymph nodes, the carcinogenic risks of radiation to the breast, and the continued statistical superiority of survival rates after total mastectomy leave the clinician with little alternative.[11] It seems apparent that total mastectomy will remain the preferred method for treating breast cancer for some time to come.[12-15]

All of this patient's allegations against her physician are subject to reasonable debate and rebuttal. But they could probably have been more easily dismissed or wholly avoided if a prompt revisit had been scheduled.

References

1. Editorial: Radiation-induced breast cancer. *Br Med J* 1(6055):191, 1977
2. Rogers JV, Powell RW: Mammographic indications for biopsy of clinically normal breasts: Correlation with pathologic findings in 72 cases. *Am J Roentgenol Radium Ther Nucl Med* 115:794, 1972
3. Shore RE, Hempelmann LH, Kowaluk E, et al: Breast neoplasms in women treated with X-rays for acute postpartum mastitis. *J Natl Cancer Inst* 59:799, 1977
4. Simon N, Silverstone SM: Radiation as a cause of breast cancer. *Bull NY Acad Med* 52:741, 1976
5. Ackerman LV, Katzenstein AL: The concept of minimal breast cancer and the pathologist's role in the diagnosis of "early carcinoma." *Cancer* 39:2755, 1977
6. Egan RL: Breast biopsy priority. Cancer versus benign preoperative masses. *Cancer* 35:612, 1975
7. Smith JA III, Gamez-Araujo JJ, Gallager HS, et al: Carcinoma of the breast: Analysis of total lymph node involvement versus level of metastasis. *Cancer* 39:527, 1977
8. Black MM, Leis HP, Kwon CS: The breast cancer controversy. *JAMA* 237:970, 1977
9. Rosen PP, Fracchia AA, Urban JA, et al: "Residual" mammary carcinoma following simulated partial mastectomy. *Cancer* 35:739, 1975
10. Shah JP, Rosen PP, Robbins GF: Pitfalls of local excision in the treatment of carcinoma of the breast. *Surg Gynecol Obstet* 136:721, 1973
11. Urban JA: Partial mastectomy: Unproved treatment for patients with potentially curable breast cancer. *Clin Bull* 3:123, 1973
12. Fisher B, Montague E, Redmond C, et al: Comparison of radical mastectomy with alternative treatments for primary breast cancer. A first report of results from a prospective randomized clinical trial. *Cancer* 39:2827, 1977
13. Forrest APM: Conservative local treatment of breast cancer. *Cancer* 39:2813, 1977
14. Maisin HE, Braeken G, Wambersie A, et al: Comparison of results of radiotherapy and radiosurgical treatment of breast cancer, stages I and II. *Radiol Clin Biol* 42:177, 1973
15. Veronesi U, Banfi A, Saccozzi R, et al: Conservative treatment of breast cancer. A trial in progress at the Cancer Institute of Milan. *Cancer* 39:2822, 1977

16

Breast cancer and estrogens

A 48-year-old woman received injections of estrogen irregularly, but at least five or six times a year, for several years. Oral estrogens were also administered. She was uncooperative and reluctant to undergo thorough examination of her breasts and pelvis. Therefore, she received only one comprehensive physical examination—performed after four years of estrogen therapy. One year later, during which she continued on estrogens but had no further examinations, a centrally placed, subareolar cancer of the left breast was diagnosed. A radical mastectomy was performed; 6 of 18 axillary lymph nodes contained metastases. A bilateral oophorectomy was performed and a regimen of chemotherapy started. At the time of review, three and a half years following surgery, the patient was alive and well without evidence of recurrent cancer. Suit was filed, alleging delay in the diagnosis of cancer and the administration of medication without adequate follow-up physical examinations.

Discussion and comment. Numerous epidemiologic and clinical observations suggest that estrogenic hormones may contribute to the development of breast cancer and also influence the rate of growth of already established cancers.[1-3] Nonetheless, the relationship between cancer of the human breast and the administration of estrogenic hormones is still debatable.[4,5] The subject has undergone intense laboratory study and clinical trial with no definitive answer.[2,7-9] Although the preponderance of scientific evidence seems to lean away from a causal relationship, the practicing physician is exposed when one of his patients who has been receiving estrogens develops a breast cancer.

In this case, the physician was in especial jeopardy because he had prescribed these drugs casually and had not insisted on thorough physical examinations of the critical target organs—the breasts and uterus—for four long years. Adherence to the simple rule of regular examinations of patients receiving hormones would have done much to mitigate the charges in this case.

References

1. Hoover R, Gray LA, Cole P, et al: Menopausal estrogens and breast cancer. *N Engl J Med* 295:401, 1976
2. Kirschner MA: The role of hormones in the etiology of human breast cancer. *Cancer* 39:2716, 1977
3. Lewison EF: Role of exogenous estrogens. In *Risk Factors in Breast Cancer. New Aspects of Breast Cancer* (Stoll BA, ed), pp 67-70. London: Heinemann Medical Books, 1976
4. Longcope C, Pratt JH: *Breast Cancer and Estriol Dynamics,* pp 62-63. San Antonio: Program of the Breast Cancer Task Force, Division of Cancer Biology Diagnosis, National Institutes of Health, 1975
5. Talwalker PK, Meites J, Mizuno H: Mammary tumor induction by estrogen or anterior pituitary hormones in ovariectomized rats given dimethylbenzanthracene. *Proc Soc Exp Biol Med* 116:531, 1962
6. Pearson OH, Molina A, Butler A, et al: Estrogens and prolactin in mammary cancer. In *Estrogens, Target Tissues and Neoplasia* (Dao TL, ed), Chicago: University of Chicago Press, 1972
7. Arthes FG, Sartwell PE, Lewison EF, et al: Breast cancer estrogens and the pill. *Proc 11th Int Cancer Cong (Florence, Italy),* 1974
8. Fasal E, Paffenbarger RS: Oral contraceptives as related to cancer and benign lesions of the breast. *J Natl Cancer Inst* 55:767, 1975
9. Casagrande J, Gerkins V, Henderson BE, et al: Exogenous estrogens and breast cancer in women with natural menopause. *J Natl Cancer Inst* 56:839, 1976

17

Male breast cancer and gynecomastia

A 54-year-old man complaining of swelling of the right breast of two months' duration consulted his physician, a board-certified internist. The swelling was associated with a 1-cm lump beneath the margin of the areola at a radius of three o'clock. It was solitary, slightly tender, firm, and freely movable, without skin dimpling. The opposite breast was normal, as were the testes. A general physical examination was unremarkable. A presumptive diagnosis of idiopathic gynecomastia of the right breast was made, and the patient was examined at regular intervals over the next 15 months. The lump and breast remained unchanged for 12 months; throughout this period the right axilla was thought to be unremarkable and there was no evidence of enlarged lymph nodes.

Fifteen months following the initial examination, nipple retraction was noticed. A breast biopsy revealed infiltrating duct carcinoma, and a modified radical mastectomy was performed. Two of 20 axillary lymph nodes were positive for metastasis: one at the apex of the axilla, the other in the lower axillary tissue. Postoperative X-ray therapy and chemotherapy were given. The patient developed disseminated skeletal metastases 18 months following surgery. Suit was filed, alleging failure to make a timely diagnosis of cancer.

Discussion and comment. Gynecomastia is probably the most common form of male breast disease; lipomas are the most frequent tumors of the male breast. Therefore, the diagnosis of gynecomastia in this patient was reasonable. In retrospect, however, the history and physical findings don't appear typical of gynecomastia. Persistence without fluctuation or change over a long period is unusual.[1-4] Gynecomastia typically is a moderately firm, diffuse breast swelling with the so-called disc sign directly beneath the areola.[2] The disc is usually a freely movable, unattached, rounded area of hardness in the subareolar zone, but symmetrically and concentrically placed.

In gynecomastia the hard area is rarely eccentric, as it was in this patient, or felt beneath a margin of the areola. Tenderness is usually but not invariably present.

In all, the picture suggests that earlier biopsy to rule out cancer would have been wise, especially before the classical and serious sign of nipple retraction became apparent.[5-7] It's conceivable, of course, that what is interpreted as gynecomastia alone can be associated with an occult cancer. Or a cancer may develop later during the course of a gynecomastia. This is very rare, and I've never seen it reported.[2] In the usual case of idiopathic, unilateral gynecomastia, it is not difficult to rule out cancer on clinical examination alone. Nevertheless, differentiation by biopsy should always be kept in mind.

The male breast is composed of rudimentary, blunt ducts and poorly developed acini.[4,5,8,9] It contains much less fat than the female breast, so the nipple and areola are closer to the ductules and the underlying pectoral fascia. It may therefore be argued that skin dimpling and nipple retraction are not actually as late a sign of male breast cancer as they are now assumed to be in female breast cancer.

In my experience, the prognosis of male breast cancer is considerably poorer than the prognosis of female breast cancer. Cortese and Cornell,[10] however, reported good results in patients whose axillary nodes were negative for metastases, noting that almost 60 per cent of patients with positive nodes survived for five years or longer. And Holleb et al[6] stated that 80 per cent of the patients with negative nodes in their series survived five years. In contrast to other reports,[6,7,10-14] my results following orchiectomy for inoperable and metastatic male breast cancer have been disappointing.

Fewer than 1 per cent of all breast cancers occur in men, and they represent 0.7 per cent of all cancers in males.[3] Even though rare, however, male breast cancer must be kept in mind. Since gynecomastia is the most common male breast complaint, the physician may have an ideal opportunity to diagnose a clinically early breast cancer without undue delay. A breast nodule in the male is unusual; if it isn't gynecomastia, the chances are good that it's malignant.

References

1. Brandao C, Torres P, Alves J: Carcinoma of the male breast: Report of 12 cases. *Folha Med* 64:255, 1972
2. Personal communications.
3. Schottenfeld D, Lillenfeld MA, Diamond H: Some observations on the epidemiology of breast cancer among males. *Am J Public Health* 53:890, 1963

4. Wilson RE: The breast. In *Davis-Christopher Textbook of Surgery* (Sabiston DC, ed), 11th ed, pp 624, 631, 658. Philadelphia: Saunders, 1977
5. Crichlow RW: Carcinoma of the male breast. *Surg Gynecol Obstet* 134:1011, 1972
6. Holleb AI, Freeman HP, Farrow JH: Cancer of the male breast. *NY J Med* 68:544, 656, 1968
7. Treves N, Holleb AI: Cancer of the male breast: A report of 146 cases. *Cancer* 8:1239, 1955
8. Crichlow RW: Breast cancer in males. *Breast Dis Breast* 2:12, 1976
9. Rubin P: Editor's comment: Male breast cancer. Current cancer concepts, multidisciplinary views; carcinoma of the breast. American Cancer Society with permission from JAMA, p 54, 1967
10. Cortese AF, Cornell GN: Carcinoma of the male breast. *Ann Surg* 173:275, 1971
11. Horn Y, Roof B: Male breast cancer: Two cases with objective regressions from Calusterone ($7\alpha,17\beta$-dimethyltestosterone) after failure. *Oncology* 33:188, 1976
12. Hudson MJK, Smart CJ: Carcinoma of the male breast. *Br J Surg* 61:440, 1974
13. Huggins C Jr, Taylor GW: Carcinoma of the male breast. *Arch Surg* 70:303, 1955
14. Panettiere FJ: Cancer in the male breast. *Cancer* 34:1324, 1974

18

Bilateral breast cancer and pregnancy

A 30-year-old woman consulted her obstetrician early in the first trimester of pregnancy. She complained of some "bumpiness" in each breast, and physical examination revealed clumped masses of tissue in both breasts, consistent with early pregnancy changes and without anything suggesting neoplasia. Seven months later she was delivered of a healthy boy. Between the initial visit and delivery, three prepartum examinations were performed, each by a different physician. The patient's breasts were examined only once during this period, at the last visit, when they were said to be normal. The medical records are poor. Four months after delivery both breasts suddenly grew more enlarged, with marked, diffuse hardness beneath each nipple and areola. Biopsies revealed cancer in each breast, and bilateral modified radical mastectomies were performed. None of the axillary nodes contained metastases. The patient underwent chemotherapy and was alive and well 20 months following surgery. Suit was filed against all four physicians who saw the patient prepartum, alleging delay in the diagnosis of breast cancer.

Discussion and comment. Cancer of the breast in pregnant women was formerly thought to carry a very poor prognosis. The older literature reported survival rates under 10 per cent, even as low as 5 per cent.[1-5] Now it's recognized that the prognosis is better than had been supposed: Not all pregnant patients who contract breast cancer die of their disease, nor do all patients under 30 years of age.[2,6,7] This patient, however, seems to have had three strikes against her: She was young, she was pregnant, and her disease was bilateral.

Younger people are expected to resist the development of malignant disease more easily than older people. When they do get cancer, therefore, their prognosis is generally poorer. It isn't known, because of sketchy prenatal care and record keeping, whether this young patient's nutritional status might have contributed to her lack of resistance to development of the disease. The fact that her baby was born healthy suggests that the mother was adequately nourished during her pregnancy. And the absence of metastases to the axillary lymph nodes improves her prognosis.

Breast cancer in pregnant women is still difficult to cure. It isn't known whether its virulence is due to the intense hormonal stimulation directed at the breasts during pregnancy, to the increased vascularization of the breasts, or to masking of the disease by the normal breast changes that occur in pregnancy.

Bilateral, simultaneous breast cancer carries a worse prognosis than unilateral disease[8] because there are not one but two sites from which it can disseminate. The outcome depends on the evidence of spread of the disease in either breast.[9]

With all these factors working against her, it's unlikely that the patient would have survived her cancer no matter when it was diagnosed. Yet 20 months after surgery she was alive and well, certainly exhibiting good resistance to the disease. There was no evidence of metastases to the lymphatic system. Probably, then, the cancer formed as late as the third trimester of pregnancy, and then rapidly "blossomed" during the postpartum period.

In this case, it's the poor quality of prenatal care and the failure to keep adequate records that expose the physician to malpractice liabilities. Despite the patient's poor prognosis, she probably didn't get cancer until late in her pregnancy, when diffuse malignant disease of both breasts would have been extremely difficult to detect. Therefore, the charge of delay in diagnosis is faulty. But, because the patient received inadequate, poorly documented prenatal care, the charge would be very hard to disprove.

References

1. Harrington SW: Carcinoma of the breast: Results of surgical treatment when carcinoma occurred in the course of pregnancy or lactation and when pregnancy occurred subsequent to operation, 1910-1933. *Ann Surg* 106:690, 1937
2. Macdonald I: Carcinoma of the breast in pregnancy and lactation. In *Carcinoma of the Breast, Current Cancer Concepts–Multidisciplinary Views* (Rubin P, ed). New York: American Cancer Society, 1967
3. Pollack RS: *Treatment of Breast Tumors,* pp 16, 90. Philadelphia: Lea & Febiger, 1958
4. Taylor GW: Carcinoma of the breast in young women. *N Engl J Med* 215:1276, 1936
5. White TT, White WC: Breast cancer in pregnancy; report of 49 cases followed five years. *Ann Surg* 144:384, 1956
6. Peters MV: The effect of pregnancy in breast cancer. In *Prognostic Factors in Breast Cancer* (Forrest APM, Kunkler PB, eds), pp 65-80. Edinburgh: Livingstone, 1968
7. Rissanen PM: Carcinoma of the breast during pregnancy and lactation. *Br J Cancer* 22:663, 1968
8. Robbins GF, Berg JW: Bilateral primary breast cancer. *Cancer* 17:1501, 1964
9. Wilson RE: Cancer in pregnancy and lactation. In *Davis-Christopher Textbook of Surgery* (Sabiston DC, ed), 11th ed, p 657. Philadelphia: Saunders, 1977

19

Inflammatory breast cancer and pregnancy

A 36-year-old woman, gravida 7, para 3, consulted her obstetrician for prenatal care at about her third month of pregnancy. Examination revealed nothing remarkable. Her breasts were described as slightly engorged but without masses and within normal limits. She was followed at regular intervals until delivery six months later, but throughout this period no further breast examinations were performed. The patient mentioned to her doctor that she had some left breast swelling and a lump in her armpit, but he didn't examine it. He reassured her that it wasn't unusual during pregnancy to have these signs in the breast and that they were just "milk glands." A breast examination in the hospital, immediately prior to delivery, was described as normal. A healthy girl was delivered without any complications.

At the first postpartum visit, five weeks later, the patient's left breast was found to be markedly swollen, red, hot, and hardened, and there was a firm mass in the left axilla. A course of antibiotics was given, without response. Biopsy three weeks later revealed inflammatory cancer of the breast, with highly undifferentiated cells and subdermal lymphatics widely involved with cancer. The patient was given radiation therapy. Laparotomy revealed metastases to both ovaries as well as the liver, and the ovaries were removed. The right breast, spine, pelvic bones, brain, and lungs shortly became involved, and the patient died six months after delivery. Suit was filed, alleging delay in diagnosis of breast cancer.

Discussion and comment. Inflammatory cancer of the breast is a uniformly fatal disease. But we now know that cancer of the breast during pregancy and lactation has a variable prognosis and is not the uniformly fatal condition it was once thought to be.[1-4] Breast cancer treated during the second half of pregnancy carries a much poorer prognosis than cancer treated during the first half[3] or the first six months postpartum.[5] It may justifiably be assumed, therefore, that pregnancy does stimulate the growth of breast cancer in many women,[5-7] but not to any predictable degree.

In pregnant women whose breast cancer metastasizes to the axillary lymph nodes, the disease is almost always fatal. In those patients whose axillary lymph nodes are negative, the prognosis is relatively good. The impression is growing that prognosis of breast cancer depends more on cellular biology and host resistance than on age, pregnancy, or when the diagnosis is made (see Chapter 46). Women whose nodes are negative seem to have an immunity or resistance that helps keep the disease limited to the breast or, if distant metastases have occurred, helps destroy or make them dormant. Even the exciting effects of pregnancy can't overcome their resistance, and they can be expected to survive. Unfortunately, the majority of women don't seem to have this immune factor.

It's important to separate the distinct entities of inflammatory and noninflammatory breast cancer in a pregnant woman.[8] This patient had inflammatory cancer, distinguished by pain, heat, diffuse swelling, induration, skin edema, and redness of the entire breast without a palpable tumor but with a large axillary mass. The biopsy and the acute onset also denote lymphangitis and lymphatic blockade. Pregnancy and lactation enhanced the venous engorgement that normally occurs in inflammatory breast cancer, and venous invasion by cancer cells proceeded even faster.

Prognosis in such a patient may be described as practically hopeless, although chemotherapy may be cause for optimism in the future. The volatile, hopeless nature of this form of cancer certainly mitigates liability in this case. Nonetheless, the familiar claim of delay in diagnosis, failure to diagnose, and failure to be thorough makes the physician's exposure all too apparent.

References

1. Holleb AI, Farrow JH: The relation of carcinoma of the breast and pregnancy in 283 patients. *Surg Gynecol Obstet* 115:65, 1962
2. Macdonald I: Carcinoma of the breast in pregnancy and lactation. In *Carcinoma of the Breast, Current Cancer Concepts–Multidisciplinary Views* (Rubin P, ed). New York: American Cancer Society, 1967
3. Peters MV: The effect of pregnancy in breast cancer. In *Prognostic Factors in Breast Cancer* (Forrest APM, Kunkler PB, eds), pp 65-80. Edinburgh: Livingstone, 1968
4. Rissanen PM: Carcinoma of the breast during pregnancy and lactation. *Br J Cancer* 22:663, 1968
5. Wilson RE: Cancer in pregnancy and lactation. In *Davis-Christopher Textbook of Surgery* (Sabiston DC, ed), 11th ed, p 657. Philadelphia: Saunders, 1977
6. Pollack RS: *Treatment of Breast Tumors*, pp 16, 60. Philadelphia: Lea & Febiger, 1958
7. White TT, White WC: Breast cancer in pregnancy; report of 49 cases followed five years. *Ann Surg* 144:384, 1956
8. Wilson RE: Inflammatory carcinoma. In *Davis-Christopher Textbook of Surgery* (Sabiston DC, ed), 11th ed, p 643. Philadelphia: Saunders, 1977

20

The lungs

Failure to discover that the plaintiff was suffering from lung cancer is frequently the charge in malpractice suits. Who's getting sued? Roentgenologists and internists head the list, although all physicians whose practice includes a substantial number of routine physical examinations have cause for concern.

Until recently, the most usual plaintiff was a patient claiming that his state of health was incorrectly determined by his personal physician because of a careless or too casually performed physical examination. If the trend of recent court decisions and rulings is any index, however, the plaintiff could be someone you have never examined or even seen.

The courts have said, in effect, that when you examine a patient, you must diagnose with reasonable care and report with reasonable accuracy the state of his health. If you don't, you may have to answer in money damages. From a personal study of recent cases, the odds are about three to two in your favor that you'd defeat a claim for "reckless failure" to discover lung cancer. Those doctors who lost either hadn't adequately checked their patients for cancer or couldn't produce records to prove they had.

Among such cases, the familiar charge of negligent X-ray analysis has usually been reserved for roentgenologists. A leading trial lawyer bluntly explains why these specialists have become a prime target:

"Roentgenologists run X-ray factories. The doctor never sees his patients. It's the technician who positions the patients and takes the pictures. Once or twice a week the doctor stands in front of a viewing box with a stack of films and a stenographer. He flips through the films like a deck of cards, sees that his reports are mailed, and then sends out his bills."

Such callous comments obviously don't apply to most roentgenologists. They reveal a total ignorance of the practice of diagnostic radiology. Yet they reflect an attitude shared by some plaintiffs' attorneys. That attitude could result in a process server's appearing at your office with a summons someday. The reason is that roentgenologists are not the only ones under fire when erroneous X-ray analysis is the complaint. If the patient was referred, the referring doctor may also be sued. One attorney put it this way:

"A doctor who refers a patient is guilty of malpractice if he knows the man he sends his patient to doesn't practice good medicine. Right now I'm suing two doctors, a family practitioner and an internist, for that."

The doctor who takes and reads his own X-rays may also be exposed to malpractice charges. He may be a board-certified internist with a subspecialty in cardiology, or board-certified in family practice, but he is not a certified diagnostic roentgenologist. When a lung cancer is overlooked, he's understandably very vulnerable. The emotional overlay of cancer on an already misinterpreted X-ray film makes this a particularly difficult position to defend.

For the general or family practitioner who practices in a rural community miles from a board-certified radiologist, taking his own X-rays is understandable and even laudable, but his exposure, though mitigated by circumstances, is still very real. Unfortunately, when errors in interpretation of X-rays are made by a physician who isn't a board-certified radiologist, he's usually held to the same standards as a board-certified specialist.

21

Lung cancer in a young man

A 40-year-old man consulted his family physician because of pain overlying the right anterior chest wall. It extended downward toward the abdomen. There was minimal discomfort in breathing, but he had an occasional cough. The patient smoked at least two packs of cigarettes a day. He was employed as a fisherman and was otherwise in good general health.

Chest X-rays, posteroanterior and right lateral, were taken and read by his own physician and declared to be negative. Three months later, because of nasal discharge and a sore throat, the patient consulted an otorhinolaryngologist. At this visit he had no accompanying cough but again complained of continued right anterior chest wall pain and now some additional midline upper back pain as well. Sinus X-rays were negative; no further X-rays were taken at that time. The nasal discharge and sore throat disappeared.

Two months later, or five months after the initial visit to the patient's family physician, his right anterior chest wall and upper back pain became severe and was now accompanied by a noticeable increase in coughing. Chest X-rays revealed widening of the mediastinum on the right and infiltration of the apical area of the right upper pulmonary lobe with destruction of the proximal portion of the right fourth rib. Further skeletal X-ray films showed an osteolytic lesion in the right iliac crest.

Biopsy of the right mediastinal mass showed a poorly differentiated adenocarcinoma consistent with origin in a lung. Brain and liver scans were negative. Radiation was given to areas of skeletal and mediastinal involvement with good relief of pain. Chemotherapy was considered in addition, but not given.[1] The patient died of cancer 11 months after definitive diagnosis. Suit was filed against both the family physician and the otorhinolaryngologist, alleging delay in the diagnosis of lung cancer that led to death of the patient.

Discussion and comment. Primary lung cancer, which was considered a rare disease 40 years ago, today accounts for most cancer deaths in males.[2-4] Despite encouraging reports on the survival rate (25 to 35 per cent five-year survival)[4, 5] and cure of lung cancer patients who undergo surgical removal of a lobe or even the entire lung, when all patients with this disease are considered the overall, all-comers survival figures are between 5 and 10 per cent.[1-3, 6, 7]

The lung cancer cell has an aggressive biology. Too often the histology is described as undifferentiated, poorly differentiated, or anaplastic carcinoma, in addition to that special, uniformly fatal entity termed an oat cell carcinoma. The reasons for a poor prognosis aren't hard to understand: the lung's highly vascular nature and a profuse lymphatic network, which offer the cancer an opportunity for early, rapid dissemination; an anatomic arrangement whereby small cancers, those less aggressive biologically, remain occult and defy detection until they spread to inaccessible sites; the complexities and inadequacies of diagnostic techniques to prove the presence of "early" cancers; and the frequency of nonmalignant lesions that cloud diagnosis of the malignant ones.

The simplistic assumption that earlier diagnosis will increase the likelihood of curing lung cancer can be challenged on the basis of the biology of the lung cancer cell alone. But even if you grant that assumption, it's apparent that early diagnosis of lung cancer can be a most elusive matter.

Chest X-rays are far from infallible diagnostic aids. Most often when lung cancer is detectable on an X-ray film, the disease is late, not early. Lung scans show the extent of a disease process more accurately than they tell us its exact nature. Bronchoscopy, bronchial washings and brushings, and sputum cytology may all confirm or strongly suggest cancer—but at what stage of the disease process?

Biopsy of lymph nodes by mediastinoscopy will aid in the diagnosis of metastatic disease, but that can hardly be called early cancer. Nor can the chief clinical manifestations of lung cancer: cough, hemoptysis, chest pain, shortness of breath, pleural effusions, enlarged cervical (supraclavicular) lymph nodes, clubbing of the fingers, hoarseness, swallowing difficulty, dizziness, headache, blurred vision, skeletal and/or rib pain, and hepatomegaly. In short, the conscientious physician may realize that cancer is present—but where? Prove it!

This patient very likely had disseminated, metastatic cancer when first seen, and his symptomatology probably was due for the most part to these metastases. Earlier diagnosis, had it been feasible, in all probability would have influenced the natural history of this cancer very little. Nonetheless, frequent serial X-rays might have been helpful diagnostic measures. If adjunctive tests (sputum cytology and so on) had also been performed, the physicians' exposure to malpractice charges would have been much less, whether or not they had led to an earlier diagnosis.

References

1. Katsuki H, Shimada K, Koyama A, et al: Long-term intermittent adjuvant chemotherapy for primary, resected lung cancer. *J Thorac Cardiovasc Surg* 70:590, 1975
2. Baum GL: *Textbook of Pulmonary Diseases,* p 773. Boston: Little, Brown, 1974
3. *Cancer Forum,* No. 12, p 144. Sydney: Australian Cancer Society, 1977
4. Sabiston DC: Carcinoma of the lung. In *Davis-Christopher Textbook of Surgery* (Sabiston DC, ed), 11th ed, pp 2124, 2137. Philadelphia: Saunders, 1977
5. Lee YTN: Prognostic factors in surgical treatment of bronchogenic carcinoma. *Surg Gynecol Obstet* 135:961, 1972
6. Bignall JR, Martin M, Smithers DW: Survival in 6,086 cases of bronchial carcinoma. *Lancet* 1:1067, 1967
7. Boucot KR, Cooper DA, Weiss W: The role of surgery in the cure of lung cancer. *Arch Intern Med* 120:168, 1967

22

Lung cancer in a young woman

A 34-year-old woman complaining of pain over the right posterior chest wall following a fall was seen in the emergency department of her local hospital. X-rays revealed linear fractures of the right eighth and ninth ribs in the back. There also was what appeared to be a patch of increased density posteriorly in the lower segment of the upper lobe of the right lung. Her chest wall symptoms cleared rapidly. She was seen twice again by her family physician and was completely asymptomatic at the time of her last visit. No further X-rays were taken.

The patient had no signs or symptoms of disease until 15 months later, when, because of cough, right posterior chest pain near the lower margin of the scapula, and a slight temperature, she returned to her family physician. Chest X-rays revealed an irregular density in about the midportion of the upper lobe of the right lung that was interpreted as a pneumonic process.

The young woman was placed on a two-week course of antibiotics. X-rays taken a month after she had completed the antibiotics suggested a regression but not total clearing of the pulmonary infiltrate. She felt better. No further investigative measures or therapy were prescribed.

She was told to return in a few weeks, but didn't. Instead, she returned three months later with an enlarged lymph node in the supraclavicular space of the right neck. Biopsy of the node showed poorly differentiated metastatic cancer consistent with bronchogenic origin. Clinical evidence of brain metastases followed shortly, and death four months later. Suit was filed against her family doctor, alleging failure to make a timely diagnosis of cancer that led to the patient's death.

Discussion and comment. A recurring issue in forensic medicine, especially where malignant disease is present, is the question of when the cancer actually started. It's almost always a matter of conjecture and leads to endless debate. In this patient an X-ray taken because of fractured ribs revealed a patch of increased density in the lower segment of the upper lobe of the right lung. What happened to that area in the lung after the rib injury is debatable; unfortunately, the inference that it represented a bronchogenic cancer that subsequently progressed is hard to rebut.

Davies[1] thoroughly reviewed the effectiveness of roentgenographic, cytologic, and other methods used to diagnose early lung cancer. Resectability was found to be approximately two times greater in patients whose cancers had been discovered by routine X-ray screening than in patients whose X-rays had been taken and cancers found after the appearance of symptoms. Although resectability cannot be considered synonymous with curability, the inference is undeniable and is a favorite tactic of plaintiffs' attorneys. The asymptomatic nature of the lung cancer appearing on the chest X-rays of this patient would have placed her in that more favorable group of patients if she'd been studied further and a definitive diagnosis of pulmonary cancer promptly made.

The problem of proving the diagnosis of lung cancer is vexing.[2] According to Rigler,[3] X-ray evidence of lung cancer is present in at least 90 per cent of patients before the onset of symptoms, but the duration from first observation of a shadow until a proven diagnosis is made took over two years in more than 50 per cent of the patients he studied. Lee,[2] in his authoritative review, thoroughly discussed the frustrations and disappointments of trying to prove the presence of lung cancer.

Fifteen months after the initial X-ray of this patient's chest, an irregular density was seen in the same general area as on the earlier film. It's tempting to conclude that the two lesions were the same. Yet 15 months is, of course, ample time for a new cancerous process to begin.

The physician is exposed because no additional diagnostic surveys of the lung were undertaken following the rib injury. Exposure is compounded by the failure to perform further investigative procedures after antibiotics failed to clear the pulmonary density completely. The patient's contributory negligence in not returning to the physician promptly, as advised, doesn't absolve him of his responsibility, but it is a mitigating factor.

Failure of antibiotics to accomplish complete clearing of a density in the lung warrants careful, thorough investigation. The doctor's position is difficult to defend from this point on, although this case certainly demonstrates the capriciousness of lung cancer: The patient was symptom-free for 15 months; the second density showed some evidence of regression following antibiotics; the patient's symptoms abated and she felt better; and there were no specific signs that clearly suggested the presence of lung cancer.

The lymph node metastasis that ultimately developed in the right supraclavicular space denotes incurable disease. Histologic examination proved it to be a highly malignant variety of lung cancer, described as poorly differentiated. This virulent form of cancer carries a poor prognosis, and cure would be doubtful no matter when the diagnosis was made. The patient's young age, 34, would tend to support this contention. When a cancer of this type shows the X-ray configuration described in the second series of chest films (15 months after the first) and also causes pain at the lower end of the scapula, dissemination has almost certainly begun and the possibility of cure is remote. Rapid spread to the lymph nodes of the neck and then metastases to the brain should come as no surprise.

This case review is an excellent example of how diagnosis of lung cancer can elude the experienced physician. Hindsight tells us that greater diligence probably wouldn't have saved the patient's life—but greater diligence might have helped the physician in court.

References

1. Davies DF: A review of detection methods for the early diagnosis of lung cancer. *J Chron Dis* 19:819, 1966
2. Lee YTN: Prognostic factors in surgical treatment of bronchogenic carcinoma. *Surg Gynecol Obstet* 135:961, 1972
3. Rigler LG: The natural history of untreated lung cancer. *Ann NY Acad Sci* 114:755, 1964

23

Cancer of the superior pulmonary sulcus: Pancoast's tumor

A 58-year-old man consulted his family doctor because of pain in the right shoulder area that extended beneath the right scapula. The pain occasionally radiated into the right posterior neck. He'd had these symptoms about four weeks and said he felt generally well otherwise. Physical examination was unremarkable. The physician took and read X-rays of the chest, posteroanterior only, and the cervicothoracic spine. They revealed some osteoarthritis of the cervical vertebrae extending from C-3 to C-7. The lungs were interpreted as being negative. The physician diagnosed cervical arthritis and placed the patient on antiarthritic medication, which afforded the patient no relief.

During the next two months, the pain increased and extended into the right axilla, with radiation toward the upper inner arm. X-rays, repeated at another institution, now showed an infiltrating density in the extreme apical area of the right lung along with evidence of erosion of the right first rib anteriorly.

Physical examination at this time revealed Horner's syndrome of the right eye, fullness and induration of the tissues of the right lower neck, and an enlarged right supraclavicular lymph node. The node was biopsied and revealed metastatic squamous cell carcinoma consistent with bronchogenic origin.

Because of the clinical and histologic findings, which proved the nature and extent of the disease, it was considered inoperable. Radiation therapy was given, with little response. The patient died six months later. Suit was filed against the family doctor, alleging delay in the diagnosis of lung cancer that led to the patient's death.

Discussion and comment. Superior sulcus cancer of bronchogenic origin (apical lung cancer) is clearly recognized as an entity today, but not too long ago was thought to be a lesion possibly separate from the lung and was termed Pancoast's tumor or syndrome.[1-4] The diagnosis of a superior sulcus tumor, uncommon as it is, should be suspected in any patient with severe, persistent pain in and around the shoulder, lower neck, and back.[1] It tends to occur in a slightly younger age group than the usual bronchogenic cancers. Diagnosis is difficult since X-rays are often obscure and misleading. Bronchoscopy is seldom informative because the tumor is located at the peripheral margins of the lung and bronchial system. Computerized axial tomography may have promise as a diagnostic aid.[5]

The origin of this form of cancer in the lung is often so occult that it takes a long time to prove that the signs and symptoms are due to a primary bronchogenic cancer occurring within the extreme apical (superior groove) segment of the lung. The lymphatics that pass through the thoracic fascia covering the apex are invaded early. Usually the cancer spreads upward and medially to involve the pleura, intercostal nerves, ribs, brachial plexus, ulnar nerve roots at C-8 and T-1, stellate ganglion, sympathetic nerve chain, and vertebrae.[1, 4] Pain in and around the shoulder girdle is a frequent initial but all-too-late symptom, since it denotes invasion of contiguous structures.

Unfortunately, tumors in the apical sulcus frequently simulate benign pleural thickenings on X-rays, but rib erosion, so often seen concomitantly, and the clinical symptoms will aid in the diagnosis.[4] Although in my experience these tumors are of the squamous cell type, the majority are anaplastic. This adds to the poor prognosis and shortens the clinical course of the disease.

Baum,[1] however, has stated that in general these tumors are low-grade squamous cell carcinomas. Their slow, relentless growth over a long period and their occult presence, which defies detection, would explain why some patients are first seen in an advanced stage of the disease, when it's too late for curative therapy.

Shaw et al[6] reported that the longest survival in untreated patients was 10 months and, in those treated with irradiation therapy, 13 months. The surgically treated patients fared only slightly better. Several authors have emphasized the value of preoperative radiation followed by en bloc resection of the ribs, vertebral margins, brachial plexus, and upper lobe of the lung.[2, 3, 6, 7] En bloc removal of this magnitude requires considerable expertise of the thoracic surgeon, and probably of the neurosurgeon who's often called in to help. Interstitial radiation is also advocated. The combination of preoperative radiation and surgical resection has been encouraging.

The superior sulcus cancer has been shown to be radioresponsive if not radiocurable. Use of radiation decreases the extent of local recurrences, prevents growth of tumor cells after dissemination, and yields higher survival rates than irradiation or surgery alone.[7]

Despite these somewhat optimistic reports, superior sulcus cancer is usually incurable. Its occult nature, diffuse spread, and tendency to involve almost all adjacent nerve structures make the disease difficult to diagnose, resect, and even palliate.

What are the pitfalls for the physician in this case? Perhaps the family physician took a risk by interpreting the patient's X-rays instead of referring the task to a roentgenologist. But the occult nature of the disease makes it likely to have been disseminated by the time the patient first complained of pain. When the medical facts are considered and the disease fully understood, the physician's exposure to malpractice would seem more apparent than real.

References

1. Baum GL: *Textbook of Pulmonary Diseases*, pp 782, 783. Boston: Little, Brown, 1974
2. Hilaris BS, Luomanen RK, Beattie EJ Jr: Integrated irradiation and surgery in the treatment of apical lung cancer. *Cancer* 27:1369, 1971
3. Hilaris BS, Martini N, Luomanen RKJ, et al: The value of preoperative radiation therapy in apical cancer of the lung. *Surg Clin North Am* 54:831, 1974
4. Sabiston DC: Carcinoma of the lung. In *Davis-Christopher Textbook of Surgery* (Sabiston DC, ed), 11th ed, pp 2129, 2132. Philadelphia: Saunders, 1977
5. Muhm JR, Brown LR, Crowe JK: Use of computed tomography in the detection of pulmonary nodules. *Mayo Clin Proc* 52:345, 1977
6. Shaw RR, Paulson DL, Kee JL Jr: Treatment of the superior sulcus tumor by irradiation followed by resection. *Ann Surg* 154:29, 1961
7. Paulson DL: The survival rate in superior sulcus tumors treated by presurgical irradiation. *JAMA* 196:342, 1966

24

The abdomen

Malpractice suits arising from abdominal surgery mishaps may or may not result in skyrocketing awards, but I've found they account for 25 per cent, perhaps even more, of all malpractice cases. There are three major hazards to guard against.

A foreign body left in the abdomen. Rarely can a surgeon successfully defend himself in court against this charge unless he can prove he took extreme precautions to prevent it. And, if all precautions are taken, foreign bodies are seldom left.

First, he can actively impress on the hospital's nurses the importance of accurate sponge and instrument counts. That, plus a personal reminder before each operation, has been shown to cut foreign body incidents significantly.

Second, the surgeon must adhere to hospital rules governing operating room procedures. A Tennessee surgeon learned that lesson when he was told to split a $40,000 judgment with a hospital for leaving a sponge in his patient's abdomen. On trial, the plaintiff's lawyer proved that the hospital's rules specifically required the scrub nurse to take an initial count and the circulating nurse to take a second count. But in this instance, he pointed out, the circulator hadn't been present to conduct the sponge count. The surgeon had sent her out of the room on an errand.

Third, if an instrument or sponge is missing and further search of the patient's abdomen would endanger his life, the surgeon can decide to record such information on his operating report and remove the article at a subsequent operation. As the United States district court in North Dakota has warned, even when the surgeon isn't negligent in losing an instrument or other foreign body, he can be held guilty of malpractice for not trying to find it when the patient's condition permits.

As a fourth malpractice preventive, a surgeon should avoid

concealing the knowledge that a foreign body has been left in a patient by a previous surgeon. If he does conceal it, and is found out, the patient can sue him for fraud.

Injury during abdominal surgery. The damages being awarded in these cases run much higher than those for foreign body claims. Most such cases can be divided into two major categories: errors in technique and accidental injuries.

When improper technique can be proved, it's apt to be expensive. A doctor in the Middle West who had operated on a bleeding peptic ulcer was ordered to pay a $150,000 judgment. The jury decided that he had improperly anastomosed the patient's stomach to the small intestine. A New York surgeon settled a malpractice case when the plaintiff's medical expert confronted him with the fact that he hadn't removed all of the patient's appendix in a prior operation. The man developed peritonitis, and it was necessary to perform additional surgery.

Accidental injuries, those that result from a slip of the scalpel or the misapplication of a clamp, can also be expensive. A New York jury told a surgeon to pay a sizable amount to a patient whose common bile duct had been severed during a gallbladder operation. The verdict was given after the plaintiff's lawyer called in a medical expert to testify for the plaintiff. In Minnesota and California, courts have held that the doctrine of res ipsa loquitur—the thing speaks for itself—applies to severed bile duct cases. Biliary surgery is no place for the inexperienced. The defendant himself has to convince the jury that he was knowledgeable and not negligent.

One surgeon was able to do just that. His patient had developed an incisional hernia following surgery for removal of gallstones. During repair of the hernia, the surgeon's scalpel made an inadvertent laceration in the small bowel, which seemed to be lying in an abnormal position. An enterocutaneous fistula developed. It was repaired at a second operation, performed by another surgeon several months later. A suit followed.

When the surgeon described in detail exactly how the accident had happened, the trial judge threw the case out of court, convinced that the perforation had occurred because of an anatomic abnormality. The judge's ruling was sustained on appeal.

Postoperative negligence. Premature discharge from the hospital is a familiar yet avoidable claim. Unfortunately, utilization review doesn't help matters, nor does the high cost of hospitalization. In areas where there's a shortage of hospital beds, rapid turnover is a prime objective.

A surgeon was sued after he authorized the discharge of a

cholecystectomy patient. A nurse had assured him by telephone that the man's incision was no longer draining. When the patient arrived home, the incision opened. Complications developed and the patient died. No patient should be released from a hospital without proper examination by his attending surgeon or by someone equally qualified.

Falls from hospital beds are an all-too-frequent cause of suits charging negligence following abdominal surgery. Unlike some of the older beds, newer hospital beds have siderails that are easily raised and locked. Most hospital rules require siderails to be raised for all sedated, postoperative, obstetric, and elderly patients. Still patients continue to roll out of their beds, rupture incisions, and sue their surgeons.

A leading New York cancer surgeon had to split a settlement with the hospital when his 67-year-old patient fell out of bed and ripped the sutures of her celiotomy incision. The hospital's rules specified siderails not only for patients over 65 but for all postoperative patients. The surgeon, however, had neglected to reinforce those rules by putting a personal order on the patient's chart.

Infection is another risk especially applicable to abdominal surgery. An Ohio surgeon paid a settlement to an appendectomy patient when she developed a secondary infection in the operative wound. The operation required removing an inflamed appendix and purulent accumulation in the abdomen. The surgeon assumed that his assistant would order an antibiotic; the assistant thought the surgeon would. Although there's no guarantee that an antibiotic will prevent infection, its use in this sophisticated age has become expected. The case was settled even before a subpoena was served.

There's another major malpractice hazard that applies to all areas of the body but is especially serious in the abdomen. It comes under the heading of rare and esoteric disease. More and more suits are being brought by those perplexing, frustrating patients whose disease defies detection until too late, who have no symptoms until the pathology is advanced, who don't have signs typical of their disease, or whose disease is so rare or unlikely that it can reasonably be discounted. Sometimes the clinical picture is so confusing that no logical course of action can be taken. Because diagnostic tests either aren't available or are imperfect, the condition is overlooked. In many such cases, differences of opinion exist and the responsible physician must make decisions on the basis of presumptive evidence only. Luck plays a large role in those decisions.

These are the patients who try the physician's soul. In them the bitterness over the malpractice issue reaches its zenith.

25

Appendicitis and pregnancy

A 24-year-old woman, gravida 4, para 3, was admitted to the hospital two days prior to delivering a normal, full-term infant. At the time of admission she complained of mild abdominal discomfort and slight, diffuse crampiness throughout her abdomen. On examination there were no areas of localized abdominal tenderness or guarding. Delivery proceeded uneventfully. Twenty-four hours following delivery, her temperature rose to 101°F and she complained of diffuse abdominal pain with beginning distention. She then revealed that she hadn't had a bowel movement for the previous six days. It was also noted that there was no passage of stool from the rectum during labor and delivery.

The patient's temperature dropped slightly on the second postpartum day but rose again on the third postpartum day. A white blood count taken on the third postpartum day was 33,000 with a predominant shift to the left. Surgical consultation was requested on the fourth postpartum day. Examination revealed a distended, diffusely tender abdomen without rigidity or localization. The patient's temperature was 100.8°F. The following day, the fifth postpartum, the patient had two somewhat watery bowel movements and her abdomen was slightly less distended and not rigid. The white blood count continued in the same range. A four-quadrant abdominal tap was performed and revealed pus in the right lower quadrant. A beta CAT scan of the abdomen suggested the presence of an intra-abdominal abscess and/or fluid collection primarily in the right lower and right upper quadrants. The patient looked poorly. Celiotomy was recommended and revealed multiple areas of abscess formation within the loops of the small intestine (mesenteric abscesses) as well as a large right lower quadrant abscess and a generous amount of purulent abdominal fluid. The appendix had ruptured and left only a gangrenous base attached to the cecum.

Residual appendectomy was performed, followed over the next seven weeks by two additional operations for drainage of intra-abdominal abscesses. Recovery was eventually complete after three months. Suit was filed, alleging failure to diagnose appendicitis with resulting prolonged morbidity.

Discussion and comment. True appendicitis is rare during pregnancy. It occurs once in every 1,000 pregnancies but is the most commonly seen extrauterine condition that requires abdominal surgery during pregnancy.[1] Its mortality rate is five times higher in the last three months than during the first six months. Fortunately, it's more common during the first two trimesters.[1] Even though it isn't unusual for pregnant women to complain of pain in the appendiceal area when they don't have appendicitis, the possibility of appendicitis should be kept in mind.[2] Suppurative peritonitis caused by a perforated appendix is much more serious during pregnancy than in the nonpregnant state. The causes of this are fairly obvious and are well described by Greenhill:

> 1) Protective adhesions are less likely to form and the omentum and intestines are pushed away by the enlarging uterus. 2) The inflammation is more stormy because of the intense vascularity of the uterus. 3) Thrombosis and phlebitis are more common. 4) Suppuration takes place higher in the abdomen (true of late pregnancy), which portion is less resistant than the lower part. 5) Drainage is less free, due to the large uterus, and abscesses burrow deeply in all directions. 6) Obstructive symptoms arise earlier. 7) Bacteria in the blood may lodge in the placenta and even in the fetus, causing abortion and infection.[3]

As this patient's case shows, the contracting uterus may cause an attached, inflamed, abscessed appendix to rupture, especially during the third stage of labor, when the corpus makes its greatest excursions.[3] Also, the diagnosis of appendicitis in the puerperium is difficult to separate from puerperal infection; the two conditions can coexist.

Baer, Reis, and Arens[4] have shown how the appendix is displaced further and further upward after the third month of gestation. At the end of the fifth month it reaches the level of the iliac crest and then rotates counterclockwise, pointing horizontally, then vertically, in 60 per cent of pregnant women by the end of the eighth month. In this position purulent dissemination, especially with mesenteric abscess formation within the loops of small intestine, readily occurs. The omentum, displaced by the enlarged uterus, can't reach the area of the inflamed appendix and contain the infection. Not until a month after birth does the appendix return to its normal position. Had appendicitis with perforation occurred earlier in this patient's pregnancy and not just before or after delivery, the risk of abortion, premature labor, infection of uterine contents, and fetal death would have been considerable.[5]

Fortunately, the patient recovered fully. Her appendicitis wasn't diagnosed at an early stage, and the longer the delay in diagnosis, the higher the mortality rate. Mortality is also increased if labor sets in during an attack of appendicitis.

Diagnosis of appendicitis during pregnancy demands no special skills but can be most difficult, especially as gestation progresses. The increased abdominal laxity that occurs during pregnancy tends to minimize abdominal signs of peritoneal irritation. The problem for the physician in this case lies in the fact that the patient was observed for four full days before operation. Yet the complex clinical setting that confronted him provides justification for his judgment not to perform an earlier operation.

References

1. Condon RE: Appendicitis during pregnancy. In *Davis-Christopher Textbook of Surgery* (Sabiston DC, ed), 11th ed, p 1068. Philadelphia: Saunders, 1977
2. Cunningham FG, McCubbin JH: Appendicitis complicating pregnancy. *Obstet Gynecol* 45:415, 1975
3. Greenhill JP: *Obstetrics*, 12th ed, p 540. Philadelphia: Saunders, 1960
4. Baer JL, Reis RA, Arens RA: Appendicitis in pregnancy with changes in position and areas of normal appendix in pregnancy. *JAMA* 98:1359, 1932
5. Thomford NR, Patti RW, Teteris NJ: Appendectomy during pregnancy. *Surg Gynecol Obstet* 129:489, 1969

26

Retrocecal appendicitis and brain abscess

A 53-year-old woman was seen by her family physician in the emergency department of a local hospital late at night. She complained of abdominal pain of six hours' duration, located mostly in the right upper quadrant. She'd had some nausea and loss of appetite, but no vomiting, and passed a slightly diarrheic stool with much flatus earlier that day. A board-certified general surgeon was immediately called in consultation.

On examination the patient appeared tense but in no acute distress. There was tenderness on the right side of the abdomen, with slight guarding, more in the upper quadrant than the lower, without rigidity, rebound, or right costovertebral tenderness. Peristaltic sounds were present but thought to be hypoactive. Rectal examination elicited nothing, but the patient cooperated poorly and the examination was felt to be inadequate. The white blood count was elevated to 11,000, with a mild shift to the left. Urinalysis was negative. The patient's temperature was slightly above 100°F. She was admitted for observation and study with a presumptive diagnosis of acute cholecystitis.

The patient's condition remained essentially unchanged the following day. She was maintained on intravenous feedings and given ampicillin empirically. A gallbladder X-ray series, performed early on the second day of admission, showed no uptake of dye. She was scheduled for a double-strength-dose cholecystogram the following day. But later the second day her white count rose to 16,000 and the shift to the left became marked. She had a chill and her temperature rose to 102°F. Her abdominal pain increased and was still most severe in the right upper quadrant. She was taken to surgery the evening of the second hospital day.

A subcostal incision was made. The gallbladder had several adhesive bands surrounding it but was normal. Exploration in the right lower quadrant revealed a retrocecal abscess collection from a perforated appendix. The appendix was removed, the stump inverted, the abdomen drained through a stab wound, and the subcostal incision, which had been extended slightly downward, closed. The patient did well postoperatively, although a purulent collection was noted in the suprafascial space of the wound on the fourth postoperative day. It was drained without incident and she continued to improve.

On the morning of the seventh day after surgery, the patient experienced a sudden plethora of neurological signs and symptoms: spontaneous right foot clonus, nausea, disorientation, drowsiness, headache, slightly blurred vision, slurred speech, and difficulty in walking. She became incontinent of bowel and urine.

A clinical diagnosis of brain abscess was made. Electroencephalography, radionuclide brain scan, arteriography, and CAT scan all supported this diagnosis. Additional angiograms, however, suggested occlusive vascular disease of the right distal internal carotid artery and the right vertebral artery. Aggressive antibiotic treatment was started. Because the patient improved, anticipated intracranial surgery was not performed; nor were brain aspirations. Thus the diagnosis remained in doubt. Residual serious neurologic defects persisted. These were mostly in the form of hemiparesis and increased in severity over the ensuing months. The patient died 10 months later.

At autopsy, the neuropathologist reported multifocal, small, old cortical encephalomalacic lesions bilaterally; ischemic bilateral encephalomalacic lesions in the cerebellum; and patchy arteriosclerosis of the circle of Willis, with total, old occlusions of the vertebral arteries.

The suit filed against the surgeon alleged that delay in the diagnosis and treatment of appendicitis had contributed to the likelihood of brain abscess, leading to the patient's death.

Discussion and comment. The contention that the patient's death in this case was due to the aftereffects of a brain abscess is not substantiated by the autopsy findings. There's more evidence that occlusive arterial disease, especially of the right internal carotid and right vertebral arteries as well as the vessels of the circle of Willis, was the causative factor leading to death. Yet hematogenous spread from a ruptured retrocecal appendicitis as a possible source of brain abscess is a consideration, remote though it may appear.[1-3]

Patients with a brain abscess uncomplicated by meningitis usually have no systemic signs of infection. The lesion may actually be occult. Skull X-rays, electroencephalograms, brain and CAT scans, cerebral angiography, and pneumoventriculograms merely show an intracranial mass that must be differentiated from a tumor, hematoma, or other space-occupying lesion.[3,4]

Hematogenous spread of infection to the brain from some other site in the body is uncommon except when it comes from the lungs or heart or when congenital defects of the heart permit paradoxical emboli from other body areas.[3] Brain abscesses that occur in this manner are most often found in areas supplied by the middle cerebral artery, the vessel that accounts for a large proportion of the brain's blood supply.[2, 3]

Intracerebral abscesses are usually single but may be multiple. As the abscess develops, it often passes through three stages. The first is acute encephalitis without pus. This is very likely synonymous with what is termed cerebritis, that stage of focal cerebral inflammation that immediately precedes the development of a brain abscess.[2-4] In the second stage, pus appears but is not well defined or walled off. In the third stage, localization with a well-defined wall takes place. There are, of course, rapidly fatal abscesses that don't pass through these three stages but appear as spreading, suppurative encephalitis.[5, 6]

This case illustrates the well-known, frequently observed difficulty of diagnosing retrocecal appendicitis. Since the clinical picture was one of acute cholecystitis, earlier diagnosis could have been made only by treating acute cholecystitis in the same fashion as acute appendicitis, i.e., by immediate surgery. This has been advocated but has fewer adherents now than in the past.[7-9]

A retrocecal abscess as the cause of a brain abscess must be a very rare complication indeed. Hematogenous brain abscesses may occur in any situation,[1, 2, 4-6, 10, 11] but beyond question are most often seen following otic infection. In these patients the abscesses are usually situated in the middle or posterior part of the temporal lobe or in the cerebellum. Brain abscesses occur with some frequency in cases of lung abscess with empyema and in patients with acute infective endocarditis. They also arise from other sources, such as osteomyelitis or even a simple boil or cutaneous sepsis. Rarely is the primary abscess in the liver. The presence of congenital heart disease would make osteomyelitis, cutaneous sepsis, or liver abscess a much more plausible primary site, as a retrocecal ruptured appendix would also be.

The case at hand leaves substantial doubt that a brain abscess ever occurred. Autopsy did not corroborate such a diagnosis. On the contrary, both angiography and autopsy showed much evidence of compromised cerebral circulation due to atheromatous vascular occlusive disease, even though the patient was only 53 years old. The sudden appearance of neurological signs and symptoms on the seventh postoperative day also doesn't suggest a brain abscess, since brain abscesses of hematogenous origin often develop slowly and the symptoms and signs appear more gradually.[4] Because aspiration of pus from within the brain wasn't attempted, nor craniotomy performed, there's a substantial lack of evidence of brain abscess.[10]

This patient was treated for her presumed abscess with heavy doses of antibiotics. They were enough to overcome her immediate difficulties, but not enough to prevent the later brain damage that ultimately led to her death. It may be argued that if a brain abscess did occur, the initial symptoms and signs were caused by cerebritis or acute encephalitis without pus formation. Antibiotic treatment at that stage could have caused resorption of the infected area. Attractive as this possibility may sound, it doesn't easily fit the actual pattern of events and clinical findings. Medical evidence appears to be lacking in the plaintiff's allegations.

References

1. Editorial: Brain abscess. *Br Med J* 5982:504, 1975
2. Walshe F: *Diseases of the Nervous System*, 11th ed, p 91. Baltimore: Williams & Wilkins, 1970
3. Wilkins RH: Intracranial infections. In *Davis-Christopher Textbook of Surgery* (Sabiston DC, ed), 11th ed, pp 1488-1489. Philadelphia: Saunders, 1977
4. Walton JN: *Brain's Diseases of the Nervous System*, 8th ed, p 431. Oxford: Oxford University Press, 1977
5. Beller AJ, Sahar J, Praiss I: Brain abscess: Review of 89 cases over a period of 30 years. *J Neurol Neurosurg Psychiat* 36:757, 1973
6. Victor M, Banker BQ: Brain abscess. *Med Clin North Am* 47:1355, 1963
7. Carey LC, Catalano PW: Acute cholecystitis. In *Davis-Christopher Textbook of Surgery* (Sabiston, DC, ed), 11th ed, p 1271. Philadelphia: Saunders, 1977
8. Coyne MJ, Schoenfield LJ: Gallstone disease. *Postgrad Med* 57:153, 1975
9. Glenn F: Trends in surgical treatment of calculous disease of the biliary tract. *Surg Gynecol Obstet* 140:877, 1975
10. LeBeau J, Creissard P, Harispe L, et al: Surgical treatment of brain abscess and subdural empyema. *J Neurosurg* 48:198, 1973
11. Samson DS, Clark K: A current review of brain abscess. *Am J Med* 54:201, 1973

27

Pylephlebitis and hepatic portal vein gas

An obese, 48-year-old man had a sudden episode of generalized abdominal pain and vomiting. His temperature rose shortly to 101°F and was followed by a shaking chill. Later that evening his temperature rose to 104°F and he had repeated chills throughout the night. The abdominal pain, not severe in the first place, had diminished slightly by the time his family physician examined him, 12 hours later. He had no signs of any intra-abdominal disease. He was started on tetracycline orally, kept at bed rest, and watched closely. Fever, chills, malaise, and weakness continued over the next two days, and he was admitted to the hospital.

On admission, the patient appeared ill. His white count was 15,000 with a marked shift to the left; his abdomen was protuberant but relaxed, with no localizing signs or tenderness; he did not complain of abdominal pain. There was a very slight suggestion of right upper quadrant tenderness, and one examiner thought his sclerae appeared faintly jaundiced. His serum bilirubin was reported to be 2.8. Flat films of the abdomen and chest taken on admission were unremarkable.

Over the next two days the patient's condition worsened, although the physical findings were essentially unchanged. A gallbladder X-ray series taken on the second day of his hospital stay showed the startling picture of hepatic portal vein gas (HPVG). The serum bilirubin had increased to 4.6; a blood culture taken the same day ultimately showed *Escherichia coli.* (One later blood culture also showed *Clostridium perfringens.*) Abdominal examination showed no change, and surgery was withheld on the grounds that there were no localization or catastrophic signs. A reasonable diagnosis simply could not be made.

By the third hospital day, the patient's condition worsened drastically. Septic shock was apparent, with concomitant renal failure, despite massive use of antibiotics and stimulation with diuretics. There were still no localized or specific abdominal signs, and this, plus his shocklike state, made surgery inadvisable. The stormy course continued, and HPVG was repeatedly visualized.

After two weeks, the patient's condition improved enough to permit abdominal exploration and drainage of an apparent liver abscess. Surgery revealed a ruptured appendix whose tip was buried in an almost fixed abscess collection situated transversely across the abdomen and buried beneath the mesosigmoid! A subphrenic abscess, liver abscess, and mesenteric abscesses were also present. His postoperative course was stormy, and in spite of all resuscitative efforts and management he died 20 days later. Suit was filed against the family physician, alleging failure to diagnose appendicitis.

Discussion and comment. The dreaded complication of pylephlebitis (portal vein pyemia, portal vein thrombophlebitis, suppurative pylephlebitis) is well recognized as a sequela of a ruptured appendix and appears frequently in the older literature.[1] With the advent of antibiotics and the more rapid diagnosis and surgery of appendicitis, pylephlebitis is seen less frequently, but it's estimated to occur in 3 per cent of ruptured appendices.[2] Sophisticated vascular surgical techniques and the attention currently given to acute obliterative disease of the mesenteric vessels means that this complication is not infrequently seen in mesenteric artery occlusion and resulting bowel necrosis.[3] Of course, pylephlebitis has numerous other causes; I refer you to further studies.[4-7]

The presence of gas in the portal vein was first reported in 1955[8] in infants and shortly thereafter recognized in adults.[3] Its peripheral distribution and configuration in the liver make it relatively easy to diagnose and differentiate from biliary tract gas, which is centrally situated within the liver. HPVG is obviously an ominous sign; it's felt to be 90 per cent fatal. There are, however, sparse reports of survival.[5, 6, 9]

The implication of HPVG is undeniable: a gangrenous, necrotic abscess collection along the tributaries of the portal vein. A review of cases of survival reported in the literature suggests, although not conclusively, that because the superior mesenteric vein's drainage is more direct in its course to the liver, infections along this venous system are more often fatal than those along the inferior mesenteric channels. In recent reports of survival, the majority of patients had gas in areas drained by the inferior mesenteric vein and its tributaries.[5-7, 9] This implies that infection of the liver will be more overwhelming in areas drained by the right side of the portal circulation or the superior mesenteric vein. HPVG almost always seems to occur in association with necrosis, distention, and congestion. The origin of the gas isn't known exactly, although it's probably due to enteric organisms that gain access to the vascular system through a damaged bowel wall. It's also possible that gas itself escapes into the mesenteric and portal veins through a bowel wall defect produced by distention, impaired circulation, vascular occlusion, and resultant necrosis.[10]

Pylephlebitis can, of course, occur without gas, and thereby with less risk of liver abscesses. Gas can only promote the development of multiple liver abscesses. The diagnosis of pylephlebitis is very difficult to make unless HPVG is seen or unless it's considered on the basis of clinical findings when no HPVG is present. Repeated chills and high fever, as occurred in this patient, are strong evidence for pylephlebitis.

Operation as early as possible would seem to be indicated to remove the insulting source of contamination. But when the primary source remains occult and the patient is in a deteriorating, shocklike state, surgery will certainly result in death. Supportive management, antibiotic therapy, and close study to find the most likely cause of the patient's condition are all that can be done. A desperately sick patient can usually withstand only one operation; specific knowledge beforehand helps make it the correct one. The dilemma confronting patient, family, and physician in the presence of overwhelming infection is all too clearly illustrated in this case.

References

1. Hoffman HL, Partington PF, DeSanctis AL: Pylephlebitis and liver abscess. *Am J Surg* 88:411, 1954
2. Condon RE: Complications of appendectomy. In *Davis-Christopher Textbook of Surgery* (Sabiston DC, ed), 11th ed, p 1078. Philadelphia: Saunders, 1977
3. Fred HL, Mayhall CG, Harle TS: Hepatic portal venous gas. *Am J Med* 44:557, 1968
4. Dodds WJ, Stewart ET, Goldberg HI: Pneumatosis intestinalis associated with hepatic portal venous gas. *Am J Dig Dis* 21:992, 1976
5. Giustra PE, Killoran PJ, Morse EK: Postoperative bowel necrosis with portal vein gas. *Am J Gastroenterol* 64:140, 1975
6. Gold RP, Seaman WB: Splenic flexure carcinoma as a source of hepatic portal venous gas. *Radiology* 122:329, 1977
7. Graham GA, Bernstein RB, Gronner AT: Gas in the portal and inferior mesenteric veins caused by diverticulitis of the sigmoid colon. *Radiology* 114:601, 1975
8. Wolfe JN, Evans WA: Gas in the portal veins of the liver in infants. A roentgenographic demonstration with postmortem anatomical correlation. *Am J Roentgenol* 74:486, 1955
9. Paciulli J, Jacobson G: Survival following roentgenographic demonstration of gas in the hepatic portal venous system. *Am J Roentgenol* 99:629, 1967
10. Goldstein WB, Cusmano JV, Gallagher JJ, et al: Portal vein gas. *Am J Roentgenol* 97:220, 1966

28

Traumatic pancreatitis

A 24-year-old man sustained severe blunt trauma to the upper abdomen in an automobile accident and was immediately taken to his local hospital. He was not in shock. The region of the xiphoid process and epigastrium was tender, but bowel sounds were present and the abdomen was soft although slightly distended. X-rays revealed fractures of the right wrist, right patella, and the anterior portion of the right 11th rib, without evidence of pneumothorax, hemothorax, or pneumoperitoneum. The patient had severe contusions and lacerations over his face, scalp, arms, and legs. His general condition remained good after prompt treatment of the fractures and lacerations, and his cardiovascular system was stable. No retroperitoneal or mesenteric bleeding was apparent. A perforated viscus seemed unlikely.

Over the next 48 hours, the patient tolerated oral fluids in small amounts but was given no solid food. His abdominal distention increased, as did upper abdominal pain and tenderness. Intravenous fluids were continued.

Abdominal distention progressed, but the decision to perform abdominal arteriography was postponed.[1, 2] The patient's abdominal discomfort increased and his temperature rose to 102°F. His hemoglobin level showed a drop from 12.5 gm on admission to 10.5 gm. His white blood count, unchanged since admission, remained slightly above 12,000. There was no discernible shift to the left. Observation was continued.

The patient's condition began to show some deterioration on the sixth day following admission. His hemoglobin had dropped further to 8.8 gm, and his white blood count had increased to 15,200. Serum and urinary amylase studies, performed for the first time, showed 300 and 400 Somogyi units, respectively. Four-quadrant paracentesis was not helpful. His abdominal distention continued, along with upper left quadrant pain, but he was still passing flatus. Abdominal X-rays showed that the transverse colon appeared to be displaced upward. Although the patient was tolerating some oral fluids and said he felt better, his falling hemoglobin and increased white count were cause for concern. A laparotomy was performed on the seventh day after admission.

The operative findings revealed a normal intestinal mesentery and no laceration of the liver or spleen. Scanty intraperitoneal fluid and soapy-looking fat necrosis (saponification) of the tissues overlying Gerota's fascia on the left, over the gastrocolic ligament, and overlying the head, body, and tail of the pancreas were found, but no active leakage of pancreatic fluid was seen. The entire pancreas was enlarged and swollen. The body of the pancreas was elevated or raised slightly from the underlying vertebrae, with evidence of hematoma formation in the area behind the pancreas, but with no active bleeding at the time. Some old blood was seen at the inferior margin of the pancreas, but no pancreatic laceration or tear was found. The diagnosis of pancreatitis was substantiated, the abdomen closed without drainage, and the patient sent to the intensive care unit in satisfactory condition.

Appropriate fluids, antibiotics, and blood and electrolyte replacement were given postoperatively. The patient's general condition was stable for the first five days after surgery, but his pulse continued to be rapid. On the morning of the sixth postoperative day, he took a sudden downward turn. The incision felt hard and firm, the abdomen painful. A repeat serum amylase was over 600 mg/100 ml, and blood glucose 220 mg/100 ml. Supportive measures were continued. The patient's condition deteriorated further. He died on the eighth postoperative day.

Autopsy revealed a tear in the middle of the posterior surface of the pancreas. Retroperitoneal and intraperitoneal hemorrhage was present and was presumed to have been caused by traumatic rupture of the pancreas with pancreatitis.

Suit was filed against the admitting physician, who had initially seen him in the emergency department, alleging delay in the diagnosis of pancreatitis with delinquent medical care that led to the patient's death.

Discussion and comment. The complex nature of this patient's problem is apparent. Expert opinions will vary because of the very nature of the underlying disease, traumatic pancreatitis. The majority of pancreatic injuries are due to penetrating wounds of the abdomen, but the dangers of blunt trauma are being recognized more and more.[2-5] The anatomic relationships of the pancreas make it an extremely difficult organ to treat; its digestive and endocrine functions only compound the difficulties. The most appropriate remark one experienced surgeon can make to another who's called upon to handle pancreatic disease is "You have my sympathy."

The fixed retroperitoneal position of the pancreas, its approximation to other organs and the aorta, vena cava, and mesenteric and splenic vessels, to name a few, and its sanguinous and rather friable nature make it a most unlikely subject for a surgical exercise. In addition to all this, the pancreas is difficult to reach, visualize, and expose thoroughly. When pancreatic hemorrhage isn't found or hasn't proved fatal, the physiologic functions of this most vexing of all abdominal organs will often apply the coup de grace.

The primary concern with traumatic pancreatitis is whether operation is necessary. Although the diagnosis of pancreatitis following blunt trauma to the abdomen was probably suspected, surgery was withheld for a week following this patient's emergency admission to the hospital. His condition stabilized following management of numerous other injuries. He was treated expectantly with fluid replacement, attention to urinary output, observation of cardiorespiratory and gastrointestinal systems, and routine laboratory and X-ray studies. On this regimen he did well for several days, but a falling hemoglobin and packed cell volume, increasing white blood count, elevated temperature, labored respirations, and further abdominal distention were indications for laparotomy. The operative findings were conclusive evidence of pancreatitis with previous hemorrhage.

Serum and urinary amylase values weren't obtained until late in the patient's hospital course, despite the presence of upper abdominal tenderness noted on admission. Nor was four-quadrant abdominal paracentesis employed until considerably after admission, along with amylase determination of the fluid. Increased serum amylase in itself need not be an indication for surgery, nor is surgery necessarily indicated even when the diagnosis of traumatic pancreatitis is clinically apparent.[3, 4]

The decision to explore the abdomen following blunt trauma is made after a progressive series of signs and symptoms: distention, increasing tenderness, a falling hematocrit, diminihed urinary output, and general changes in vital signs.[2, 4-7] As this case shows, isolated pancreatic injury may give few intra-abdominal signs or symptoms. Shock, when due to proven blood loss, is the most obvious stimulus for early operation. The other signs and symptoms that convince the surgeon to operate rather than observe take time—48 to 72 hours—to develop. Indeed, with nonpenetrating trauma to the pancreas, an occasional patient may be asymptomatic for even weeks or months until a pseudocyst occurs or distal pancreatitis develops because of a ductal stricture.[3]

Surgical treatment of this patient is where the greatest difficulty lies. Recent surgical experience and detailed studies favor certain methodologies in the management of traumatic pancreatitis.[1, 2, 4, 8-10] Soapy-looking fat necrosis (saponification) is an indication of pancreatic rupture and a ductal leak. A hemorrhagic collection behind the pancreas indicates previous or current pancreatic bleeding. At operation this patient, after what appears to have been adequate exposure of the pancreas, had no evidence of active bleeding or leakage of pancreatic fluid. Nonetheless, several approved therapeutic measures could have been done at that time:

1. After exploring the site of hematoma collection, insert drains, preferably of the sump type, into the area of hemorrhage to provide external drainage of the damaged tissue.
2. Remove a portion of the tail of the pancreas to the point of injury, i.e., close the proximal end of the pancreatic duct and resect the portion of the gland to the left of the traumatic transection.
3. Resect some portion of the pancreas and anastomose it and its duct to the small intestine; i.e., make an interposed Roux-en-Y loop.
4. Drain the common bile duct and perform a jejunostomy.
5. Perform a pancreaticoduodenectomy, especially if the pancreatic duct has ruptured.

Since the disease process appeared stabilized and self-controlled, the surgeon elected to do nothing. Manipulation of what seemed an early edematous pancreatitis or a spontaneously sealed simple bleeding site might have created a violent hemorrhagic pancreatitis, changing an expected mortality of about 10 per cent to 90 per cent. This very real possibility is thought-provoking.

The complicated nature of traumatic pancreatitis and the difficulties encountered in its management make dogmatic statements, especially with the aid of hindsight, unwise and unjustified. Management of the patient with pancreatitis is an individual matter where the extent of involvement and the circumstances at the time play decisive roles.[6] Perhaps this explains the differing opinions about its treatment. There's consensus,[5, 8-10] however, that when pancreatic necrosis is present, some form of drainage—biliary T-tube or general abdominal—may be helpful. The trend in the management of pancreatic injuries is toward more aggressive surgery in order to avoid the almost certain complications of pancreatic duct rupture and hemorrhage this case illustrates so well. On-the-scene evaluation does much to explain and support difficult surgical decisions that turn out adversely. There are occasions when even classical measures advocated in authoritative texts are simply inappropriate or impossible.

References

1. Freeark RJ, Shoemaker WC, Baker RJ: Aortography in blunt abdominal trauma. *Arch Surg* 96:705, 1968
2. Meyers HL: The radiologic evaluation of patients with nonpenetrating abdominal trauma. *Surg Clin North Am* 48:1205, 1968
3. Bradley EL, Zeppa R, Warren WD: The pancreas. In *Davis-Christopher Textbook of Surgery* (Sabiston DC, ed), 11th ed, pp 1287-1304. Philadelphia: Saunders, 1977
4. Donovan AJ, Turrill F, Berne CJ: Injuries of the pancreas from blunt trauma. *Surg Clin North Am* 52:649, 1972
5. Jones RC, Shires GR: Pancreatic trauma. *Arch Surg* 102:424, 1971
6. Foley WJ, Gaines RD, Fry WJ: Pancreaticoduodenectomy for severe trauma to head of pancreas and associated structures. *Ann Surg* 170:759, 1969
7. Sturim HS: The surgical management of pancreatic injuries. *Surg Gynecol Obstet* 122:133, 1966
8. Berne CJ, Donovan AJ, White EJ, et al: Duodenal "diverticulization" for duodenal and pancreatic injury. *Am J Surg* 127:503, 1974
9. Nance FC, DeLoach DH: Pancreaticoduodenectomy following abdominal trauma. *J Trauma* 11:577, 1971
10. Zinner MJ, Baker RR, Cameron JL: Pancreatic cutaneous fistula. *Surg Gynecol Obstet* 138:710, 1974

29

Duodenal perforation

A 31-year-old woman received injury to the upper abdominal wall during an automobile accident. The dashboard of the car in which she was riding struck her just below the costal margins, in the epigastric area. She was wearing a lap seat belt, but not a shoulder strap. Her family physician examined her several hours later and noted only mild upper abdominal soreness and backache. He admitted her to the hospital. X-rays of the abdomen were negative without evidence of free air; spine and rib films showed nothing significant. The following day she developed an ileus with nausea and vomiting, an elevated white blood cell count of 14,000 with a shift to the left, fever to 101°F, and a drop in hematocrit. Her urinary output began to diminish. Intravenous fluids, nasogastric suction, and supportive measures were continued.

Over the next three days the patient's condition was relatively unchanged with no specific abdominal signs. On the fourth day following admission, her hematocrit dropped further, white count increased, fever rose, and her abdomen showed distention with beginning tenderness and guarding, more noticeable in the right upper quadrant. Urinary output was extremely scant. Surgical consultation was requested. Peritoneal lavage was performed, with the return of essentially unremarkable fluid. By the sixth day her condition further deteriorated and laparotomy was performed.

The operative findings revealed free, purulent fluid within the abdomen with scattered abscesses throughout, dilated loops of small intestine, and a large abscess collection in the right lower abdomen below the pelvic brim. The picture was that of a perforated viscus. The small and large intestines were "run" from the ligament of Treitz downward, but no perforation was found.

There was no grayish-black swelling beneath the retroperitoneal layer in the area of the duodenum to suggest hemorrhage, and no crepitus, which would suggest perforation, was noted. The stomach, duodenum, and pancreas appeared unremarkable. There was no sign of splenic or hepatic bleeding.

Postoperatively the patient did poorly. She ran a septic course with increasing renal failure and further signs of intra-abdominal abscess collection. A gastrointestinal study was performed on the second postoperative day (eighth day of hospitalization) and revealed a leak of barium from the third portion of the duodenum. Another operation was performed six hours later. The abscesses were drained and an attempt was made to close the perforated duodenum. The perforation was longitudinal, not transverse. The patient continued to do poorly, ran an increasingly toxic, septic course with ensuing complete renal shutdown, and died three days later.

The pertinent finding at autopsy, in addition to multiple intra-abdominal abscesses, was a 2-cm longitudinal perforation of the third, or transverse, portion (the hidden portion) of the duodenum along its inferior, posterior, antimesenteric, and retroperitoneal borders. The sutured area of the duodenal closure had opened. Slight retroperitoneal hemorrhage was evident. Suit was filed against the surgeon and family physician, alleging failure to diagnose intestinal perforation and peritonitis.

Discussion and comment. Duodenal perforation following blunt upper abdominal trauma is often clinically occult; symptoms are apt to be delayed for hours or days. Furthermore, its incidence is relatively rare; intraperitoneal rupture due to blunt trauma accounts for fewer than 10 per cent of duodenal perforations.[1, 2] These factors frequently cause the surgeon or diagnostician to overlook the possibility of an occult perforation in the hidden, posterior, retroperitoneal portion of the duodenum.[3-6] The fact that the duodenum lies in the depths of the upper abdomen, covered by the liver's edge and protected anteriorly by the costal margins and posteriorly by the vertebral column, only adds to the complexity of diagnosing perforations, since that protection also masks symptoms. A small perforation of the retroperitoneal surface gives pitifully few clinical signs or symptoms. In this patient, despite complete perforation, symptoms were mild to lacking for four days following the injury. The fact that there was no associated pancreatic injury only enhanced the subtle nature of the perforation.[7, 9] Diagnosis was necessarily delayed.

Surgery performed more than 12 hours following complete perforation of this portion of the duodenum generally ends fatally.[2-4, 6, 9] On X-rays, complete duodenal rupture usually shows retroperitoneal air bubbles along the upper border of the psoas muscle on the right side or around the perirenal fat line.[2] The upper part of the psoas muscle on the right side is blunted and obliterated, with some scoliosis of the lumbar spine to the left. Yet such signs were lacking in X-ray studies of this patient. The gastrointestinal X-rays, which unfortunately weren't performed until the eighth hospital day, were specific and very valuable in proving the presence and location of a duodenal perforation.

Blunt abdominal trauma that affects the duodenum may cause hematoma formation within the duodenal wall without perforation, or a serosal tear without complete perforation.[10] The lack of symptoms in this patient suggests that one of these possibilities occurred initially and progressed after several days to complete perforation with resulting leakage. This, however, is conjectural.

When surgery is performed, the possibility of duodenal perforation must be kept in mind and the entire duodenum mobilized to the ligament of Treitz.[1, 2, 4, 11] Most perforations of the duodenum following blunt abdominal trauma are transverse, but this one was longitudinal. If an intramural hematoma is found, it should be evacuated with proper closure (transverse if possible) of the bowel wall. Gastrojejunostomy, vagotomy, antrectomy, and other drainage procedures have their places in the management of this complex problem, and their use will vary with the extent of injury.

Decompression of the duodenal lumen is important postoperatively and can be aided by a nasogastric tube passed through a gastrojejunostomy or by tube duodenostomy, tube jejunostomy, or nasogastric suction through the pylorus into the duodenum. With associated pancreatic injury, T-tube choledochostomy is advisable.

When the pancreas is involved, although it wasn't in this patient, several difficult decisions must be made.[7, 8, 12] Appropriate measures range from simple drainage of the area by soft rubber tubes or subcapsular hematoma evacuation and drainage through incision of the peritoneum overlying the pancreas, to pancreaticoduodenectomy for the fractured pancreas. Pancreaticoduodenectomy is an especially important consideration if pancreatic duct rupture has occurred (see Chapter 28).

The chain of events as they unfolded in this patient is typical of that seen following blunt duodenal injury without pancreatic involvement. The overall mortality even in the best of hands is about 30 per cent. The critical factor in mortality is a delay of over 24 hours from the time of injury to the time of surgical repair. Intra-abdominal abscesses, mesenteric and subphrenic, septic shock, renal failure, and death are the sequelae. The malpractice exposure in this case was enhanced by an eight-day delay in diagnosis, but it's difficult to see how the diagnosis could have been made earlier.

References

1. Harrison RC, Debas HT: Injuries of the stomach and duodenum. *Surg Clin North Am* 52:635, 1972
2. Roman E, Silva YJ, Lucas C: Management of blunt duodenal injury. *Surg Gynecol Obstet* 132:7, 1971
3. Cleveland HC, Waddell WR: Retroperitoneal rupture of the duodenum due to nonpenetrating trauma. *Surg Clin North Am* 43:413, 1963
4. Davis J J, Cohn I Jr, Nance FC: Diagnosis and management of blunt abdominal trauma. *Ann Surg* 183:672, 1976
5. Donovan AJ, Hagen WE: Traumatic perforation of the duodenum. *Am J Surg* 11:341, 1966
6. Ritchie WP Jr, Ersek RA, Bunch WL, et al: Combined visceral and vertebral injuries from lap type seat belts. *Surg Gynecol Obstet* 131:431, 1970
7. Kerry RL, Glas WW: Traumatic injuries of the pancreas and duodenum. *Arch Surg* 85:813, 1962
8. Lucas CE: Diagnosis and treatment of pancreatic and duodenal injury. *Surg Clin North Am* 57:49, 1977
9. Foley RW, Harris LS, Pilcher DB: Abdominal injuries in automobile accidents: Review of care of fatally injured patients. *J Trauma* 17:611, 1977
10. Freeark RJ, Norcross WJ, Corley RD: Operation for obstructing duodenal hematoma. *Surg Clin North Am* 46:85, 1966
11. Cattell RB, Braasch JW: Technique of exposure of the duodenum. *Surg Gynecol Obstet* 111:378, 1960
12. Heitsch RC, Knutson CO, Fulton RL, et al: Delineation of critical factors in the treatment of pancreatic trauma. *Surgery* 80:523, 1976

30

Pancreatitis, pancreatic abscess, and pseudocystenteric fistula

A 44-year-old man was seen by his family physician because of recurring attacks of upper abdominal pain of four days' duration. The patient was a known alcoholic, and a diagnosis of chronic relapsing pancreatitis had been made over the previous three years. During that period he'd had about five or six attacks of abdominal pain, which subsided in 10 to 20 days after each hospitalization. Clinical and laboratory studies were always consistent with the diagnosis of pancreatitis.

During this particular exacerbation, the history revealed severe upper abdominal pain with some radiation to each flank area. Pain also penetrated through to the back. The patient experienced nausea, had vomited several times during the previous 72 hours, and noticed abdominal distention. The epigastrium was tender to palpation; the abdomen was not rigid, but guarding was present. In the upper abdomen, to the left of the midline, a large, firm, smooth mass was felt, mildly tender to the pressure of palpation. There was no jaundice or discoloration of the skin of the flanks (Grey Turner's sign) or periumbilical discoloration (Cullen's sign).

High serum and urinary amylase levels were recorded, as well as serum and urinary lipase. The patient ran a low-grade temperature and had a white count of 14,000 with a slight shift to the left.

X-rays of the abdomen revealed some calcifications, presumably within the pancreas, which had been noted on films a year before. A large, upper midabdominal, cystlike mass was seen with a dilated loop of what was probably atonic small intestine. The stomach, on lateral films, was pushed anteriorly and upward by the cystic tumor. The tumor had air and fluid levels within it.

Ultrasound was not employed.[1] The patient stabilized well on supportive treatment: nasogastric suction, intravenous fluids monitored by a central venous pressure line, blood gases to alert against respiratory failure, relief of pain with minimal dosages of morphine and meperidine (Demerol), and antibiotics. When his general condition improved sufficiently, a right transfemoral selective visceral (celiac, hepatic, splenic, and superior mesenteric) arteriogram was obtained. It showed an avascular area in the body and tail of the pancreas. It was thought to be a large pseudocyst, filled with air and fluid levels, as the X-rays had shown earlier.

Over the next few days the patient's abdomen was examined by palpation alone. Although the cyst seemed to grow smaller, it persisted. A surgeon was called in consultation. Operation was recommended, and the patient was taken to surgery four days later. At operation a still-large pancreatic pseudocyst was found, extending anteriorly and upward from the body and tail of the pancreas. The "cyst" had spontaneously ruptured into a loop of jejunum through a 5-mm opening that formed an autoenteric fistula and had partially drained itself. It was not infected, and there was no evidence of hemorrhage.

The surgeon made a broad, new, suture anastomosis between cyst wall and jejunum, side to side, in the area of spontaneous rupture of the cyst, after trimming back to good tissue on the cyst wall. A jejunojejunostomy was also made below this. Dependent drainage was believed to have been obtained. A gastrotomy was also performed to see if any of the cyst had ruptured into the stomach. It had not. No gallstones were present. The abdomen was simply drained.

The patient did remarkably well postoperatively, had no complications, and was discharged in a little over two weeks. His abdominal pains persisted, however, as did his alcohol intake. Nausea, vomiting, indigestion, and bloating occurred as before. He remained chronically ill. He was kept under observation and examined periodically. Abdominal examination revealed no recurrence of the cyst. Again, ultrasound to follow the progression or complete regression of the cyst was not employed.

Eight months following surgery, the patient was readmitted to the hospital as an acute emergency and seen by the same physicians. He had severe abdominal pains, a high fever, a white count of over 17,000, a cough, some shortness of breath, and back pain. He appeared toxic and was slightly jaundiced. The cyst was not palpable. Supportive therapy was begun, but he failed to respond. X-rays of the abdomen revealed multiple small gas bubbles in the left upper quadrant, retrogastric and believed to be extraenteric, the so-called soap bubble sign.[2] His condition suddently deteriorated even further, his temperature rose, and all laboratory observations were consistent with sepsis. Within 24 hours he became comatose and died.

Autopsy revealed a massive, purulent abscess in the right lobe of the liver, a subphrenic abscess extending downward along the right peritoneum to the pelvis, a large, right pleural effusion, and an abscess collection in the lesser peritoneal sac involving the body and tail of the pancreas. The cystenteric anastomosis was secure and fibrosed and the cyst was collapsed. Suit was filed against the family physician and the surgeon, alleging delay in the diagnosis of pancreatic and liver abscesses leading to the patient's death.

Discussion and comment. The relentless nature of pancreatitis in some patients, whether acute, chronic, or chronic relapsing, is vividly portrayed in this patient. His alcoholism was not controlled—and the well-established clinical association of this disease with chronic alcoholism is common knowledge. Alcohol affects the pancreatic cells directly. Yet it doesn't cause the cirrhotic effect seen in the liver.[2] This might be a factor of duration of the disease, since pancreatitis seems to have a shorter natural history than cirrhosis.

More germane to this case is the difficulty of its successful management and therapy. Pseudocysts of the pancreas may occur any time after an attack of pancreatitis.[3] As a rule, six weeks after the cyst forms, its fibrous wall will be firm enough to hold suturing. The success of internal drainage by anastomosing the cyst to a segment of jejunum, preferably with a Roux-en-Y procedure, or to the stomach, depends to a large degree on whether the cyst wall is tough enough to hold sutures. Dependent drainage of the cyst, as with any drainage procedure, is important.

Surgical outpouching, or marsupialization, of pancreatic pseudocysts should always be considered, especially when pancreatic abscesses are present or when the cyst is infected. I've never been fortunate enough to find a pancreatic cyst small enough or with loose enough attachments to the surrounding structures to be thoroughly excised.

Spontaneous perforation of a pseudocyst into the stomach or, as in this patient, into the jejunum must occur in very rare instances.[2, 4, 5] Enteric-abscess fistulization is known to occur in patients with a pancreatic abscess.[6] When the spontaneous opening that forms between pseudocyst and intestinal tract is inadequate for satisfactory drainage, and the cyst persists, surgery is indicated.

There's some evidence that these spontaneous fistulas will tend to close by themselves.[4] Therefore, in order to obtain adequate drainage, a wide surgical anastomosis must be made between jejunum and cyst wall. A side-to-side (cyst wall-to-jejunal wall) union is preferable. Bradley et al,[2, 4] have carefully described the advantages of a Roux-en-Y anastomosis, which not only permits good drainage but also tends to exclude the cyst from the small intestinal stream. The jejunojejunostomy performed on this patient would, theoretically at least, also have aided in excluding the cyst.

The preoperative finding of air within a cyst is, of course, highly suggestive of spontaneous perforation into some portion of the gastrointestinal tract. Air may also mean superimposed infection and abscess formation within the pseudocyst. Surgery is indicated for a pseudocyst with or without infection or abscess, and drainage is a must. Fortunately, spontaneous rupture of a pseudocyst is rare, probably occurring in 5 per cent of patients.[3, 4, 7]

The pseudocyst in this case was not infected, nor was a pancreatic abscess seen at operation. The patient's prompt postoperative recovery supports the absence of a pancreatic abscess. Internal drainage did provide adequate resolution of the pseudocyst. Unfortunately, the recurring episodes of pancreatitis continued, ultimately with abscess formation.[7]

The fatal episode in this patient's illness clearly demonstrates the interrelationship between the pancreas and its contiguous structures, and also the relentless nature of pancreatitis. Pancreatic abscess and acute lesser sac collection seemed almost inevitable with this patient's alcoholism and recurring outbreaks of acute attacks. The rapidity with which his condition deteriorated following his last hospital admission is characteristic of pancreatic abscess.[7] The subphrenic abscess and right pleural effusions are also known to occur in pancreatitis without abscess formation.[7, 8]

How long this patient had a hepatic abscess, and when it developed, is a matter of conjecture. Such abscesses can be occult and found only at operation.[9-11] Yet recent or chronic illness, especially of this type, or past abdominal surgery is an important clinical hint. The most likely source of this patient's liver abscess was the venous drainage of the portal circulation.[5, 9, 12] The body and tail of the pancreas are drained by small veins that empty into the splenic vein and thus provide a ready source for portal vein (pylephlebitis) and liver infection from the pancreas and lesser peritoneal sac[2, 5, 12] (see Chapter 27). An adjacent septic focus, such as the subphrenic abscess, might also have been responsible.

The allegations made against the physicians do not fit the diagnostic and surgical complexities in this case. The charges were based on the simplistic idea that death was due to an abscess and could have been prevented if the abscess had been diagnosed in time. But death in this patient was actually due to overwhelming sepsis that was impossible to prevent or control and caused by one of the most difficult intra-abdominal conditions to treat. Acceptable standards of care were maintained throughout, but were inadequate to cure the disease at hand. It's difficult to find scientific evidence to fit the charges, and they ignore the true medical issues.

References

1. Gonzalez A, Bradley EL III, Clements JL Jr: Pseudocyst formation in acute pancreatitis: Experience with ultrasonic evaluation of 99 cases. *Am J Roentgenol* 127:315, 1976
2. Bradley EL, Zeppa R, Warren WD: The pancreas. In *Davis-Christopher Textbook of Surgery* (Sabiston DC, ed), 11th ed, p 1287. Philadelphia: Saunders, 1977
3. Hanna WA: Rupture of pancreatic cysts: Report of a case and review of the literature. *Br J Surg* 47:495, 1963
4. Bradley EL, Clements JL: Transenteric rupture of pancreatic pseudocysts: Management of pseudocystenteric fistulae. *Am Surg* 42:827, 1976
5. Healey JE Jr: *A Synopsis of Clinical Anatomy,* p 159. Philadelphia: Saunders, 1969
6. Miller TA, Lindenauer SM, Frey CF: Pancreatic abscess. *Arch Surg* 108:545, 1974
7. Bolooki H, Jaffe B, Gliedman ML: Pancreatic abscesses and lesser omental sac collections. *Surg Gynecol Obstet* 126:1301, 1968
8. Anderson WJ, Skinner DB, Zuidema GD, et al: Chronic pancreatic pleural effusions. *Surg Gynecol Obstet* 137:827, 1973
9. McFee AS, Franklin ME Jr, Aust JB: Pyogenic liver abscess. In *Davis-Christopher Textbook of Surgery* (Sabiston DC, ed), 11th ed, pp 1207-1208. Philadelphia: Saunders, 1977
10. Palmer ED: The changing manifestations of pyogenic liver abscess. *JAMA* 231:192, 1975
11. Pitt HA, Zuidema GD: Factors influencing mortality in the treatment of pyogenic hepatic abscess. *Surg Gynecol Obstet* 140:228, 1975
12. *Morris' Human Anatomy,* 9th ed, p 750. Philadelphia: Blakiston, 1933

31

Cancer of the body of the pancreas

A plump, 52-year-old woman consulted her family physician, a general practitioner whom she had been seeing on and off for over 20 years and in whom she had much confidence. Her chief complaints were some upper abdominal distress, slight heartburn, mild indigestion, and loss of appetite. She had voluntarily reduced her food intake, which caused some constipation, and had started to lose weight. She occasionally noticed pain in the left upper quadrant of the abdomen. A nagging backache in the lumbar area had been present for about a month.

On examination she was in no distress and looked well. The only finding was some mild tenderness in the region of the spleen, but the spleen could not be felt. A rectal examination was unremarkable. Routine laboratory studies—complete blood count and urinalysis—were negative. An upper gastrointestinal X-ray series was normal, as was a barium enema study of her colon. An orthopedic consultant could find no specific reason for the backache.

The patient was given dietary advice and relaxants and observed. There was little change over the next few weeks, but the backache persisted and pain increased in the left upper abdominal quadrant. Two months following her initial visit, she passed a tarry stool. Her indigestion, left upper quadrant pain, and backache had all worsened. She was admitted to the hospital. Gastroscopy showed a posterior wall tumor penetrating into the midportion of the stomach from behind. A biopsy revealed adenocarcinoma consistent with origin in the pancreas. This was confirmed at laparotomy. Resection was not feasible. The patient died three months later. Suit was filed against the family physician, alleging failure to make a timely diagnosis of cancer that led to the patient's death.

Discussion and comment. The dismal prognosis of cancer of the pancreas is common knowledge. Even when jaundice is present, which would at least suggest the diagnosis of cancer, the outlook is still very poor. These facts tend to dampen the enthusiasm of the experienced surgeon confronted with cancer arising in the pancreatic body and tail when no jaundice is present. Without jaundice, the cancer simply defies detection. This is unfortunate, because in some respects surgery for cancer of the body and tail of the pancreas can be easier for both patient and surgeon.[1-6]

Initial symptoms, whether the cancer is in the head or body of the pancreas, are vague, and diagnosis requires a high index of suspicion. Cancer arising in a part of the pancreas more distant from the biliary system is especially frustrating to the diagnostician. The frequently seen symptoms of cancer in the pancreatic body—abdominal pain, backache, bowel disturbance, indigestion, hematemesis, and melena—are so often late manifestations of the disease.

Diagnostic studies may be a little more helpful than outward clinical findings, but as a rule biochemical abnormalities are also minimal or absent. The secretin and secretin-pancreozymin tests might help in studying the exocrine pancreas, but are less reliable for tumors of the body and tail.[3] Carcinoembryonic antigen is not an early test for pancreatic cancer, nor does it discriminate pancreatic cancer from other cancers. Pancreatic oncofetal antigen (POA) has been found to be elevated in the serum of 50 per cent of patients with pancreatic cancer.[4] But some patients with pancreatitis have an elevated POA, as do pregnant women, some women with advanced breast cancer, some patients with bronchogenic carcinoma, and some smokers.[4] POA is in the early phases of clinical investigation, as is the study of serum ribonuclease. Cytologic studies of pancreatic secretions often are corroborative and in experienced hands can be strongly diagnostic, but are unpleasant for the patient.

Upper gastrointestinal X-ray studies can be useful in diagnosing cancer of the pancreatic head. In about one-third of patients with cancer in this area, X-rays will show widening of the duodenal C loop, the inverted 3 sign, and some evidence of external pressure against the duodenum. In my experience, however, the majority of patients who have these positive findings have inoperable disease. Unfortunately, gastrointestinal X-rays are often wholly normal with body and tail cancer. Only rarely does one see displacement of the colon, gastric wall rigidity, flattening of the antrum, and anterior displacement of the stomach with cancer of the pancreatic body.

Ultrasonography has been heralded as a helpful diagnostic aid. Computerized axial tomography provides more detailed information but is costly, involves exposure to radiation, and is sometimes unavailable. Lesions less than 2 to 3 cm in diameter are not likely to be diagnosed by ultrasonic scanning with any degree of confidence.[7, 8] Despite these most sophisticated instruments, the survival rate of patients with pancreatic cancer hasn't changed much.[4, 6, 8, 9-11] The reason is obvious: These diagnostic instruments aren't employed until symptoms arise, and when symptoms arise the cancer is often incurable.

Radionuclide scans have been disappointing diagnostic aids. Endoscopic retrograde cholangiopancreatography has high diagnostic value,[4, 12] but the ductal system must be sufficiently displaced or distorted to suggest an aberration.[9] The demonstration of a tumor blush or tumor vessels in the distribution of the pancreatic blood supply by selective visceral angiography is another diagnostic aid, but its accuracy depends on the degree of vascularization of the tumor, which is variable. Vascular irregularity in the region of the tumor (so-called encasement) was thought to be pathognomonic of cancer, but is also seen in pancreatitis.[9]

Graphic visualization of the pancreas, ductal cytology, and biochemical tests all fall short of permitting an unequivocal diagnosis of pancreatic cancer. A patient with a tumor situated in the body or tail, as in this case, usually doesn't exhibit the triad of weight loss, pain, and jaundice so often seen with cancer of the pancreatic head. That triad is the signal to perform a laparotomy,[9] but even then the majority of cancers are inoperable.[5] From the diagnostic standpoint, at any rate, cancer of the pancreatic body or tail is almost another disease.

Pancreaticoduodenectomy is the only therapy available for surgical cure of pancreatic cancer. The disease responds poorly to chemotherapy and radiation.[13] Because of the joint blood supply to the second portion of the duodenum and the head of the pancreas through the superior and inferior pancreaticoduodenal arteries, resection of the pancreatic head, as in the original Whipple operation or a total pancreatectomy, demands simultaneous duodenectomy. The location of the common bile duct, which traverses the pancreatic head, is, of course, an added reason for duodenectomy. The surgery is demanding, and results are disappointing. Whether total pancreatectomy, as opposed to the original Whipple procedure, can increase the survival rate in pancreatic cancer, head or body, is the subject of much surgical effort and study.[1, 2, 4, 9, 12, 14, 15]

The operability rate of all ductal cancers varies but is probably between 5 and 20 per cent. Hermann[4] quotes from the Commission on Professional and Hospital Activities in Ann Arbor, Michigan: "In 1969 one million patients had a diagnosis of carcinoma of the pancreas, 271 pancreaticoduodenectomies were performed with 87 deaths, an operative mortality of 32 per cent and an overall five year survival of only 4 per cent." Better survival figures are reported by others.[1, 4, 12, 14, 15] They are encouraging but still remain isolated reports.[5]

Cancer of the pancreas, whether it arises in the body and tail or in the head, bears a discouraging prognosis. With a disease so difficult to diagnose and cure, it's hard to support the charge of malpractice. In this case, especially, it appears that acceptable standards of care were not breached. The physician admitted the patient to the hospital promptly when her symptoms worsened. Unfortunately, it was late in the progress of the disease; but it's doubtful that earlier diagnosis and treatment would have improved the outcome.

References

1. Castellanos J, Manifacio G, Lillehei RC, et al: Total pancreatectomy for ductal carcinoma of the head of the pancreas: Current status. *Am J Surg* 131:595, 1976
2. Child CG, Frey CF, Fry WJ: A reappraisal of removal of ninety-five per cent of the distal portion of the pancreas. *Surg Gynecol Obstet* 129:49, 1969
3. Diamond D, Fisher B: Pancreatic cancer. *Surg Clin North Am* 55:363, 1975
4. Levin B, ReMine WH, Hermann RE, et al: Panel: Cancer of the pancreas. *Am J Surg* 135:185, 1978
5. Personal communications
6. Uhland H, Parshley PF: Obscure intussusception diagnosed by ultrasonography. *JAMA* 239:224, 1978
7. Holm HH, Rasmussen SN, Kristensen JK: Errors and pitfalls in ultrasonic scanning of the abdomen. *Br J Radiol* 45:835, 1972
8. McCormack LR, Seat SG, Strum WB: Pancreatic carcinoma. *JAMA* 238:240, 1977
9. Bradley EL, Zeppa R, Warren WD: The pancreas. In *Davis-Christopher Textbook of Surgery* (Sabiston DC ed), 11th ed, pp 1287-1316. Philadelphia: Saunders, 1977
10. Doust BD: The use of ultrasound in the diagnosis of gastroenterological disease. *Gastroenterology* 70:602, 1976
11. Sackler JP, Passalaqua AM: Diagnostic uses of ultrasound. *Postgrad Med* 60:95, 1976
12. Cohn I: Gastrointestinal cancer. *Am J Surg* 135:3, 1978
13. Ultmann JE, Stein RS, Desser RK: *Cancer Chemotherapy for Primary Physicians*, pp 25, 29. Oradell, NJ: Medical Economics Book Division, 1979
14. Hicks RE, Brooks JR: Total pancreatectomy for ductal carcinoma. *Surg Gynecol Obstet* 133:16, 1971
15. Lawrence AG, Ghosh BC: Total pancreatectomy for carcinoma of the pancreas. *Am J Surg* 133:244, 1977

32

Small intestinal lymphoma

A 53-year-old woman had been under her physician's care for 15 years, during which time he diagnosed nonspecific colitis. The patient had a long-standing history of peptic ulcer disease and also a hiatal hernia. The hernia was repaired and at the same time a vagotomy done without gastric drainage. Postoperatively the patient's gastric complaints were reduced, but she continued to have signs and symptoms of "colitis." Barium enema X-rays suggested ulcerative colitis, but repeat films showed no real evidence of this condition. She was treated supportively and got along fairly well.

During an episode of colicky pain the patient was found to have severe anemia with a normal white count and differential. She had accompanying weight loss, anorexia, and fatigue. She felt mentally depressed, but she had previously been depressed along with her peptic ulcer disease.

A thorough physical examination was negative, as was proctoscopy. Chest X-rays and a barium enema were essentially unremarkable. An upper gastrointestinal series without small bowel follow-through was reported to be negative. A bone marrow aspiration showed nothing significant. She was thought to have iron deficiency anemia and was treated accordingly.

The anemia responded poorly to medication. About four months later she was admitted to the hospital with lower and midabdominal cramps, a hemoglobin of 8.5 gm, and the suggestion of a mass in the lower midabdomen. X-ray studies of the stomach, small intestine, and colon revealed a large defect in what was probably the lower small intestine with involvement of the sigmoid colon. A chest X-ray was negative.

Operation disclosed a large tumor involving the distal third of the ileum and extending outward to the sigmoid colon, with a small area of fixation to the urinary bladder. Extension onto the small intestinal mesentery was marked. The tumor was totally resected, including the areas of fixation to the bladder and sigmoid. The ileum was anastomosed end to end. The histologic diagnosis was histiocytic lymphoma of the small intestine, ileum, and mesentery of the ileum. The lymph nodes within the mesentery were said to be negative for lymphoma.

The patient did well postoperatively. Radiation therapy was instituted after a liver biopsy, bone marrow aspiration, lymphangiogram, liver and spleen scans, and intravenous pyelogram all were found to be negative. The patient recovered remarkably and was alive and well over five years following surgery. But suit was filed, alleging delay in the diagnosis of lymphoma (cancer) with a resulting poor prognosis.

Discussion and comment. The ubiquitous disease lymphoma, when present in the small intestine, may simply defy detection.[1-3] As with so many other small intestinal tumors, its presence will go unnoticed until obstruction, intussusception (rare with lymphomas), bleeding, or, rarely, perforation occurs. The diagnosis is then made at an emergency operation.

Lymphoma is the most common small intestinal sarcoma,[4-7] but its overall incidence within the intestine is still rare. Yet the possibility of its presence, occult as it may be, should be kept in mind. The problem, as with so many other small intestinal cancers, is the lack of symptoms until the disease shows clinical progression. Even anemia, which may suggest a hidden gastrointestinal tumor, is a relatively late manifestation of the disease in my experience. Should a small intestinal tumor be suspected, X-ray studies of the small bowel, or so-called small bowel follow-through, is warranted after visualization of the upper gastrointestinal tract.

Dawson[5, 7] has suggested four criteria to establish the diagnosis of primary bowel lymphoma:

1. No generalized, superficial, or mediastinal lymphadenopathy
2. Normal white cell count and differential smear
3. Restriction to regional nodes at surgery
4. Liver and spleen free of tumor.

Since involvement of the small intestine can be either primary or part of a generalized lymphoma, it's important to distinguish between the two. Localized lymphomas of the gastrointestinal tract treated by curative resection and followed by 3,000 to 4,000 rads may have five-year survival rates as high as 85 per cent.[6] Chemotherapy may possibly add to this impressive figure.

The majority of small intestinal lymphomas occur in the ileum with the jejunum next in frequency of involvement.[4-7] The operative findings in this patient included a not uncommon characteristic of intestinal lymphoma: Its fixation to the urinary bladder and a small adjoining segment of the sigmoid was due to a peripheral inflammatory reaction and not to invasion by the lymphomatous process. Histologic study showed no lymphoma at these sites.

The disease in this patient was restricted to the small intestine and its adjacent regional mesentery, not the lymph nodes. This, along with a negative liver biopsy and bone marrow aspiration, a normal white blood count and differential smear, a negative chest X-ray (mediastinum), normal liver and spleen scans, no generalized superficial lymphadenopathy, and a negative lymphangiogram, is strong evidence that the disease process was a relatively limited primary small bowel lymphoma.

The patient's course seems to support this conclusion. Allegations of delayed diagnosis that worsened her prognosis would seem to be difficult to prove. Furthermore, it's safe to say that the confusing presence of long-standing "colitis" may very well have masked the presence of a lymphoma but, of course, had nothing to do with causing it. The wholly indefinite nature of the lymphoma's date of origin or potential for spread is also relevant. Unfortunately, "cancer" and "delay" once again become pitfalls that expose the physician to charges of malpractice.

References

1. Croome RD III, Newsome JF: Benign and malignant tumors of the small intestine. *South Med J* 61:271, 1968
2. Good CA: Tumors of the small intestine. *Am J Roentgenol* 89:685, 1963
3. Pagtalunan RJG, Mayo CW, Dockerty MB: Primary malignant tumors of the small intestine. *Am J Surg* 108:13, 1964
4. Barrowman JA, Pollock DJ, Taylor JH, et al: Small intestinal lymphoma presenting as malabsorption after vagotomy and gastrojejunostomy. *Br J Clin Pract* 30:21, 1976
5. Dawson IMP, Cornes JJ, Morson BC: Primary malignant lymphoid tumors of the intestinal tract. Report of 37 cases with a study of factors influencing prognosis. *Br J Surg* 49:80, 1961
6. Loehr WJ, Mujahed Z, Zahn FD, et al: Primary lymphoma of the gastrointestinal tract: A review of 100 cases. *Ann Surg* 170:232, 1969
7. Mason GR: Tumors of the duodenum and small intestine. In *Davis-Christopher Textbook of Surgery* (Sabiston DC, ed), 11th ed, p 970. Philadelphia: Saunders, 1977

33

Morbid obesity and jejunoileal bypass

A 28-year-old, 380-pound (173-kg) man consulted a surgeon for a weight-losing operation. The emotionally stable, affable, cooperative young man had tried almost all other forms of weight reduction without success. After careful discussion and preliminary physical examination, he was admitted to the hospital. Preoperative laboratory tests, ECG, pulmonary function studies, chest and gallbladder X-rays, and suitable bowel preparation were performed. An intravenous pyelogram was not obtained. The operation, performed three days after hospital admission, consisted of a cholecystectomy because of the presence of gallstones, an appendectomy, and a jejunoileal bypass in which 14 inches (35 cm) of jejunum were anastomosed to 4 inches (10 cm) of terminal ileum, end to end. The distal jejunum was closed and secured to the adjacent mesentery; the proximal ileum was anastomosed to the right side of the transverse colon, end to side.[1-4]

The patient's condition remained stable for the first three days following the surgery. Then, on the fourth postoperative day, his temperature rose to 104.2°F. His abdomen was crampy, generally tender, and distended; his white blood count rose to 15,000. Serum electrolytes were within the normal range. The urinary output diminished, but bowel sounds were present and the patient passed some flatus. Excessive amounts of gastric fluid were suctioned from the stomach. The high fever persisted, and urinary output decreased markedly. The white blood count remained elevated, and the tenderness of the abdomen continued. The patient looked worse, and it was suspected that peritonitis had developed.

On the sixth postoperative day he was reoperated upon. A small amount of slightly turbid, faintly purulent, yellowish fluid surrounded the jejunoileal anastomosis, but nothing else was noted that would suggest an abscess or gross peritoneal contamination. The anastomosis between the ileum and the right transverse colon appeared intact. Nonetheless, the surgeon, suspecting a leak, took down the jejunoileal anastomosis, trimmed back the margins, and reanastomosed the jejunum and ileum, end to end. At this operation a liver biopsy was performed.

The patient did poorly following the second operation, failed to respond to supportive therapy, and rapidly went into apparent hepatic and renal failure. He died three days later. Autopsy findings were not very helpful. There was some evidence of peritonitis around the jejunoileal anastomosis, but no real abscess collection was present. Some early cloudy swelling of the liver, tubular damage in the kidneys, probably tubular acidosis, and terminal bronchopneumonia without any cardiac findings were all that was found. The patient's widow filed a wrongful death action, alleging mismanagement and incompetent surgery.

Discussion and comment. The operation to relieve morbid obesity, sometimes called malignant obesity, performed either as a partial ileal bypass or as a jejunoileal bypass, is not enthusiastically favored but is nonetheless an accepted method of treating this condition. As experience with this form of surgery accumulates, especially with regard to its physiologic and metabolic aspects, it may become more commonplace. There are several modifications of the operation, all somewhat similar to what's described here.[1-6] The chief purpose of the surgery is to reduce hyperlipidemia and serum cholesterol.

The rationale for the operation has been carefully studied and developed, [1, 3, 4, 7-9] but the complications resulting from its performance have cast doubt on its usefulness.[8-12] But where adequate, sophisticated metabolic studies and control are available and in the hands of surgeons and anesthesiologists who do the procedure frequently, it's usually successful. When these essential criteria are met, an accepted standard of care maintained, and the alternatives considered, the operation may be life-enhancing. Careful selection of patients, however, is essential.

Medical consultation prior to surgery of this type is always helpful but not necessarily essential. Since endocrine reasons for obesity of this magnitude are rare, it's fair to say that consultation to rule out endocrine disorders preoperatively isn't needed.[5, 9] Obesity due to endocrine disorders usually isn't difficult to distinguish from malignant obesity. Many surgeons insist on both a medical and a psychiatric consultation before they'll agree to operate. One must candidly admit, however, that the psychiatric consult is requested more for "thoroughness" of preoperative work-up than out of actual necessity, although it would always be informative. Large bowel preparation, as well as cardiac, pulmonary, renal, and hepatic studies, are essential preoperatively and must be thorough.

Electrolyte problems often follow the operation and are aggravated by sepsis—a complication the morbidly obese are highly susceptible to.[2, 13] Electrolyte failure, although it occurred in this patient, probably was not the direct cause of death. The proximate cause of death in this case was more likely sepsis followed by renal failure, with electrolyte derangement occurring as a sequel. The electrolytes were within the normal range before the patient's kidneys started to fail as a result of septic complications.

Adequate fluid replacement is obviously required, and fluid monitoring must be constant and accurate. The kidney changes reported at autopsy are consistent with renal failure concomitant with the toxic effects of generalized abdominal sepsis.

It's best for these patients to be placed in an intensive care unit postoperatively. A good example of the value of intensive care is the prompt performance of a second operation six days after the first. This sound though difficult decision was made easier by accurate studies and close observation. The patient's clinical appearance, signs, and symptoms all suggested that intraperitoneal leakage from the jejunoileal anastomosis might be causing peritonitis. The operation proved this.

In the initial operation the jejunoileal segment was anastomosed to the colon. In other words, the operation wasn't just a jejunoileal end-to-side bypass or even a partial ileal bypass.[1-6] It was a jejunoileal bypass in which the end of the proximal jejunum was sewn to the end of the distal ileum. The distal jejunum was closed and the proximal ileum was sewn to the transverse colon. This means that when the colon was opened to make the ileocolic anastomosis, the peritoneal cavity was exposed to the potentially virulent bacteria that normally inhabit the colon—an additional reason for suspecting peritonitis.

Controversy surrounds the operation performed on this patient and similar surgery.[1,7] Should a simple end-to-side, isoperistaltic jejunoileal bypass be done, or should the bypass be performed as it was in this patient, adding an anastomosis between the small intestine and the ascending, transverse, or sigmoid colon? Experts' opinions also vary with regard to the length of the jejunoileal segment, for example. Recommendations for altering the length at a second operation have been suggested.[1-3, 5-8, 10, 11, 14]

The surgeon should be alert to long-term postoperative complications and be in a position to manage them, if possible. Diarrhea tends to disappear over three to six months, but other complications, such as electrolyte imbalance, lack of vitamin B_{12} absorption, polyarthritis, urinary calculi, hepatic decompensation, problems of the defunctionalized jejunum and bowel, obstruction by intussusception of the bypassed segment of ileum and jejunum, hair loss, and probably cholelithiasis should be anticipated. In some patients the electrolytic and physiologic response is so poor that the bowel must be returned to its normal anatomic arrangement. Jejunocolic shunt has lost favor,[6, 10] as has an ileosigmoid anastomosis.[15]

Obviously, any surgeon who performs this operation must thoroughly discuss its pros and cons with the patient beforehand. It's also clear that anyone who requests this operation would want full discussion with the physician. Few operative procedures demand more patient-physician rapport. Medical liability with these difficult problems is hard to assess.

References

1. Buchwald H, Moore RB, Varco RL: Intestinal bypass procedures for hyperlipidemia and for morbid obesity. In *Davis-Christopher Textbook of Surgery* (Sabiston DC, ed), 11th ed, p 1024. Philadelphia: Saunders, 1977
2. Scott HW Jr, Sandstead HH, Brill AB, et al: Experience with a new technic of intestinal bypass in the treatment of morbid obesity. *Ann Surg* 174:560, 1971
3. Scott HW Jr, Law DH IV, Sandstead HH, et al: Jejunoileal shunt in surgical treatment of morbid obesity. *Ann Surg* 171:770, 1970
4. Scott HW Jr, Dean RH, LeQuire V, et al: Alterations in plasma lipid concentrations in normal and hyperlipidemic patients with morbid obesity before and after jejunoileal bypass. *Am J Surg* 135:341, 1978
5. Payne JH, DeWind LT: Surgical treatment of obesity. *Am J Surg* 118:141, 1969
6. Payne JH, DeWind L, Schwab CE, et al: Surgical treatment of morbid obesity. *Arch Surg* 106:432, 1973
7. Buchwald H, Moore RB, Varco RL: Surgical treatment of hyperlipidemia. *Circulation* 49:1, 1974
8. Drenick EH, Simmons F, Murphy JF: Effect on hepatic morphology of treatment of obesity by fasting, reducing diets, and small bowel bypass. *N Engl J Med* 282:829, 1970
9. Payne JH, DeWind LT, Commons RR: Metabolic observations in patients with jejunocolic shunts. *Am J Surg* 106:273, 1963
10. Kern WH, Payne JH, DeWind LT: Hepatic changes after small intestinal bypass for morbid obesity. *Am J Clin Pathol* 61:763, 1974
11. Editorial: Liver damage after intestinal bypass for weight reduction. *Nutr Rev* 28:185, 1970
12. Maxwell JG, Richards RC, Albo D Jr: Fatty degeneration of the liver after intestinal bypass for obesity. *Am J Surg* 116:648, 1968
13. Personal communications
14. Snodgrass PJ: Obesity: Small bowel bypass and liver disease. *N Engl J Med* 282:870, 1970
15. Gourlay RH, Reynolds C: Complications of surgery for morbid obesity. *Am J Surg* 136:54, 1978

34

Crohn's disease, granulomatous colitis, and colon cancer

A 56-year-old man consulted his family physician because of lower abdominal cramps, which were stronger on the right side than the left. He also experienced some indigestion, mild weight loss, and a bloated feeling after eating. The patient judged the slight but continued diarrhea that accompanied these symptoms to be a change in bowel habit.

A thorough history was taken and a complete physical examination performed. There was some right lower quadrant tenderness, but the abdomen was soft and there were no palpable masses. A shallow anal fissure was present at the anterior margin. The patient had mild anemia, an increased sedimentation rate, and slightly lowered serum protein. The stool was negative for occult blood.

A gastrointestinal X-ray with small bowel follow-through showed narrowing and distortion of the terminal ileum (string sign), a picture thought to be consistent with the diagnosis of regional ileitis (enteritis). A barium enema X-ray of the colon suggested an area of narrowing in the right transverse colon just after the hepatic flexure, possibly representing granulomatous involvement of that portion of colon. Proctosigmoidoscopy was unremarkable except for the anal fissure, which was limited to the anal verge alone. Barium enema X-rays of the colon were repeated a few days later to evaluate the right transverse colon further, but showed nothing new.

Symptoms continued for about eight months despite medical management of the presumed regional ileitis (Crohn's disease). Since he had little relief, the patient consulted other physicians. A repeat X-ray study of the small intestine revealed not only narrowing of the lumen of the terminal ileum but also what was thought to be thickening of the bowel wall. On barium enema study of the large intestine, the area of narrowing of the right transverse colon was interpreted as probable carcinoma.

At surgery a right transverse colon cancer was proven and resected by right hemicolectomy. Twenty lymph nodes in the colonic mesentery were free of metastasis. The terminal ileum was also resected and an ileotransverse colon anastomosis made. The ileum revealed generalized ulceration and considerable granulation of the mucosa as well as numerous inflammatory cells. These findings were felt to be compatible with regional ileitis. The patient recovered nicely following surgery, but suit was filed against the original physician, alleging failure to diagnose cancer of the colon.

Discussion and comment. Because small bowel cancer in Crohn's disease is rare, an increased incidence of cancer in the involved colonic segment was not recognized until fairly recently.[1, 2] Crohn's disease is also rare, so time was needed to observe a clinically significant number of patients. Only two years after Crohn's original description of regional ileitis, it was recognized that the large bowel also can be involved in the granulomatous process.[1, 3-5] The disease process therefore no longer remains obscure.

Several recent reports [6-10] have confirmed the tendency for neoplasms to develop at the site of granulomatous disease, not only in the colon but also in the small intestine. An increased incidence of cancer has also been reported in surgically excluded segments of both large and small bowel.[6-8, 11] This implies that bypass procedures that exclude diseased segments of bowel do not protect the patient from potential malignant change in those areas. It appears increasingly clear that in granulomatous colitis (Crohn's) the risk of cancer is greater than in the general population. Patients with inflammatory bowel disease affecting the colon must be watched carefully for the development of this dangerous complication.

As this case shows, the large intestine may contain cancer even if the granulomatous, inflamed small intestine does not. Or the colon cancer may be a direct extension of cancer of the ileum or occur after an intervening segment of normal colon (skip lesion).[1, 5]

How long Crohn's disease must exist before cancer of the colon occurs is unknown.[12-14] Farmer et al[15] reported on a patient who had ileocolic Crohn's disease for 20 years. Because of intestinal obstruction, operation was performed and a carcinoma of the rectosigmoid was found in an area involved with granulomatous colitis (Crohn's). Farmer et al noted that this was the only one of 500 patients operated on for Crohn's disease in whom a carcinoma was found in an involved segment of the intestine. Certainly, at this stage of our knowledge regarding the frequency of colon cancer in granulomatous colitis or enteritis, the indications for surgery should remain conservative.[3, 5, 12-14] Yet cancer associated with inflammatory colonic disease, as suggested above, is becoming an increasingly pertinent consideration.[6, 8]

The location of the disease within the intestinal tract would seem appropriate. Krause et al [16] listed their indications for surgery in this disease but didn't mention the possibility of cancer of the colon, nor did Farmer et al [15] include it in their indications for surgery in patients with colonic Crohn's disease. At least the practicing physician should keep in mind the relationship between granulomatous colitis (Crohn's) and colon cancer and follow such patients carefully.

This case also illustrates the occult nature of right-sided colon cancer. Diagnosis was clouded by the presence of ileocolitis (Crohn's, which very likely added confusion to the early barium enema films. Regional enteritis may be only one phase of granulomatous disease of the large and small intestines. Not infrequently regions of the colon eventually become involved. The reverse—spread of the disease from colon to ileum—may also occur, although apparently far less commonly.

Whether right transverse colitis actually existed in this patient is open to question. And it can be debated whether the colitis, if it was present, was a precursor of the cancer. The allegation of failure to diagnose colon cancer must be counterbalanced by the concerted initial effort at study of the patient's colon. There was no breach in acceptable standards of care. Furthermore, the difficulty of diagnosing this form of cancer and/or colitis is apparent. Finally, doubt exists as to when the cancer actually occurred. The medical facts clarify the clinical problem and seem to refute the charges.

References

1. Drucker WR: Regional enteritis (Crohn's disease). In *Davis-Christopher Textbook of Surgery* (Sabiston DC, ed), 11th ed, pp 1018, 1019. Philadelphia: Saunders, 1977
2. Drucker WR: Regional enteritis. In *Davis-Christopher Textbook of Surgery* (Sabiston DC, ed), 10th ed, p 897. Philadelphia: Saunders, 1972
3. Goligher JC, deDombal FT, Burton I: Crohn's disease, with special reference to surgical management. *Prog Surg* 10:1, 1972
4. Price AB, Morson BC: Inflammatory bowel disease. *Hum Pathol*6:7, 1975
5. Sachar DB, Janowitz HD: Inflammatory bowel disease. *Disease-a-Month*, July 1974
6. Fishman RS, Fleming CR, Stephens DH: Roentgenographic simulation of colonic cancer by benign masses in Crohn's colitis. *Mayo Clin Proc* 53:447, 1978
7. Greenstein AJ, Sachar D, Pucillo A, et al: Cancer in Crohn's disease after diversionary surgery. *AM J Surg* 135:86, 1978
8. Hiuzenga KA: Colonic cancer in inflammatory bowel disease. *Mayo Clin Proc* 53:474, 1978
9. Kim U, Klein M, Baek S, et al: Carcinoma of the small intestine in Crohn's disease—occurrence in a bypassed loop. *Mt Sinai J Med* 43:461, 1976
10. Perrett AD, Truelove SC, Massarella GR: Crohn's disease and carcinoma of colon. *Br Med J*2:466, 1968
11. Weedon DD, Shorter RG, Ilstrup DM, et al: Crohn's disease and cancer. *N Engl J Med* 289:1099, 1973

12. Fawaz KA, Glotzer DJ, Goldman H, et al: Ulcerative colitis and Crohn's disease of the colon—A comparison of the long term postoperative courses. *Gastroenterology* 71:372, 1976
13. Lennard-Jones JE, Morson BC: Changing concepts in Crohn's disease. *Disease-a-Month,* Aug 1969
14. Thayer WR: Crohn's disease (regional enteritis). A look at the last four years. *Scand J Gastroenterol* 5(supp 6):165, 1970
15. Farmer RG, Hawk WA, Turnbull RB Jr: Indications for surgery in Crohn's disease. *Gastroenterols ogy*71:245, 1976
16. Krause U, Bergman L, Norlen BJ: Crohn's disease. A clinical study based on 186 patients. *Scand J Gastroenterol* 6:97, 1971

35

Amebic colitis and amebic liver abscess

A 38-year-old woman went to her family physician with a complaint of abdominal pain during the previous 48 hours. She was nauseated, had vomited twice, and felt sick. About six hours before the doctor saw her, the pain had settled in the right lower quadrant of her abdomen. She'd had occasional mild diarrhea without blood for the previous two weeks. The patient had enjoyed good health all her life, had never traveled beyond the continental United States, and had lived in the same house for the past 10 years. She had had no previous surgery or medical illness of significance. Her family history was unremarkable. Her two children, aged 15 and 12, were healthy, as was her husband.

Laboratory studies revealed a hematocrit of 38, a slightly elevated erythrocyte sedimentation rate, and a white blood count of 14,000 with a predominant shift to the left. Her temperature was 100.6°F. Pulse and respirations were not excessive. Stool examination revealed no occult blood and no diarrhea. A chest X-ray was essentially normal but suggested elevation of the right diaphragm.

The only pertinent physical finding on examination was right lower quadrant abdominal tenderness with some guarding and slight rigidity. Pelvic and rectal examinations were unremarkable. A presumptive diagnosis of appendicitis seemed reasonable.

At celiotomy through a right lower transverse incision, the abdomen was free of generalized contamination and intraperitoneal fluid. The only remarkable finding was in the right lower quadrant. The cecum was involved in a boggy, swollen, soft to mildly firm process that caused marked edema of its walls. The process extended outward to the adventitia. It caused edema and some redness of the proximal appendix, but the picture was clearly not that of appendicitis. The mass seemed secondary to a localized inflammation involving the cecum and a portion of the ascending colon.

The cecal mesentery contained numerous enlarged lymph nodes. There was a perforation, or through-and-through opening, approximately 2 cm across on the lateral cecal wall near its blind end. A small abscess, partly walled off by action of omental and surrounding tissues, was situated near the site of perforation. The cecum was granular, brown, and indurated. Differentiation from a carcinoma was difficult. The liver was described as normal.

A right hemicolectomy was performed with end-to-end ileo-transverse colon anastomosis. Microscopic studies showed large, necrotizing mucosal ulcers covered with a fibrinopurulent exudate within the colon. Inflammation extended through the muscularis to the outside adventitia and showed areas of organization and an exuberant granulating fibroblastic response.[1] No evidence of a specific granulomatous inflammation was found. Cancer was ruled out.

The patient did well for 48 hours but then had a stormy postoperative course. Her temperature rose to 102°F on the third and to 104°F on the fourth postoperative day. White blood cell counts remained elevated and reached 18,000; her abdomen became distended, pain in the right hypochondriac and epigastric area was continuous and severe, and respirations were labored. The patient also noticed pain in her right shoulder and base of her right neck. Her temperature continued elevated and she had chills. Palpation revealed tenderness over the liver in the intercostal spaces, but without evidence of a subcostal bulge. The liver was enlarged. A chest X-ray showed increased elevation of the right diaphragm with evidence of atelectasis, pneumonitis, and some pleurisy at the base of the right lower lobe of the lung. The patient looked toxic and severely ill.

Although the pathology report on the operative specimen didn't reveal the presence of *Entamoeba histolytica* in the tissues, the diagnosis of amebic colitis was suspected. An indirect hemagglutination test was positive for amebiasis on the sixth postoperative day. The patient was started on emetine hydrochloride and chloroquine hydrochloride intramuscularly. Metronidazole was not given, since she couldn't tolerate oral medication.

With increasing tenderness over the right hypochondrium and liver, a presumptive diagnosis of amebic hepatic abscess was made. A radionuclide image of the liver using ^{99m}Tc sulfur colloid was ordered. This technique was felt to be more useful than the more commonly used ^{67}Ga citrate. A large filling defect in the anterior superior portion of the right lobe of the liver was seen and felt to be almost pathognomic of a liver abscess.

The patient's condition deteriorated further. She was operated upon again on the seventh postoperative day for drainage of an amebic liver abscess. Unfortunately, it had already ruptured, spilling its contents throughout the peritoneal cavity and causing highly dangerous amebic peritonitis. The abscess was extensively drained and the abdomen irrigated and cleaned as thoroughly as possible. Liberal amounts of liver tissue composed of the abscess and surrounding tissue were given to the pathologist. The ileotransverse anastomosis of the prior operation appeared intact.

The pathologist's report on the liver tissue revealed granular and eosinophilic necrotic material. Amebae were seen in the periphery of the abscess material, not in the center of the necrotic debris. Surrounding hepatic cells just beyond the abscessed area appeared normal and did not contain amebae.

The patient did not recover. She died 48 hours following the second procedure. Suit was filed against the surgeon, alleging failure to diagnose colonic amebiasis with an associated liver abscess and improper indications for colon resection.

Discussion and comment. As Cohn and Nance[2] have pointed out, amebic colitis is usually a relatively mild disease and responds to medical treatment. The introduction by Powell[3] of metronidazole supplemented by oxytetracycline has been helpful. Metronidazole may be said to be the drug of choice; it should be given even when an amebic abscess of the liver is suspected but not proven. Supplemental prescription of emetine hydrochloride or chloroquine hydrochloride, which unlike metronidazole can be given parenterally (see below), aids in the medical management of this disease.[4, 5] In severe cases where both intestinal infection and hepatic abscess are present, a combination of these drugs is often necessary.

All these drugs have toxic side effects, and the patient must be carefully monitored. Metronidazole is well absorbed following oral intake and is excreted in the urine in an unchanged form. Nausea, diarrhea, slight dizziness, and occasional urine discoloration have been reported. There may be moderate leukopenia. Metronidazole is contraindicated in patients with blood dyscrasias or with active organic disease of the central nervous system.[6] It must be given orally, but an intravenous preparation has recently been reported[7] and another parenteral (intramuscular and subcutaneous) form is currently being studied. Alcohol intake should be avoided.

Dehydroemetine dihydrochloride, which in the United States is still under investigation, and the well-known emetine hydrochloride offer rapid, potent amebicidal properties in both intestines and liver. They may be given subcutaneously or intramuscularly, but not by IV. Both drugs are cardiotoxic and should be given with extreme care, if at all, to patients with cardiac or renal disease.[6] Emetine hydrochloride should be accompanied by chloroquine hydrochloride to promote destruction of any trophozoites that may have been carried to the liver. Both are given intramuscularly.

Oral amebicides include chloroquine phosphate and carbarsone. Chloroquine phosphate is readily absorbed from the gastrointestinal tract and concentrates in the liver. It has side effects: nausea, vomiting, diarrhea, headache, neuritis, psychiatric disturbances (confusion), and visual impairment. Carbarsone, an arsenic derivative, is not recommended as the initial agent or when any degree of amebic hepatitis is present. Although it's one of the most innocuous of organic arsenicals, it also has toxic manifestations. It is contraindicated in any form of other liver or kidney disease, in the presence of contracted visual or color fields, or when the patient has a history of sensitivity to organic or inorganic arsenicals.

Despite its repeated appearance in nonendemic areas, amebiasis is still relatively unusual in the United States. The global incidence has been estimated at about 13 per cent of the total population. In the United States the infestation rate is about 10 per cent but varies locally, with figures as low as 3.9 per cent.[8, 9] It therefore isn't a disease that sits uppermost in the thoughts of a surgeon confronted with an acute abdomen. In addition, the disease's severity, symptoms, and clinical course vary greatly. These factors conspire to make amebiasis a puzzling disease to diagnose unless its possibility is kept in mind.

The incubation period of amebic colitis is variable but generally long. Its onset is insidious. The course of the disease is protracted and marked by recurring episodes of dysentery alternating with periods of remission.[10] It may be symptomless or produce vague, nondescript abdominal pains with or without digestive discomfort. Asymptomatic patients actually greatly outnumber those with clinical dysentery.[10, 11]

Even when dysentery marked by bloody mucoid diarrhea occurs, the extent of colonic and rectal ulceration also varies markedly. The disease usually affects the whole colon in the acute, fulminating stage, but in the chronic, indolent phase is most often localized to the rectum. As is well known, acute amebiasis resembles ulcerative colitis.

On proctosigmoidoscopy one may, presumably in the earlier stage of disease, see scattered, pinpoint ulcers, also petechiae or yellowish elevations of the mucosa with hyperemic margins that mark the site of future ulcerations.[1] Chronic amebiasis or longer-standing disease often presents as a granulomatous proctitis (somewhat resembling syphilitic proctitis without the ulcers) and produces deep, punched-out ulcers with overhanging edges as the trophozoites penetrate into the submucosa, extend laterally in this layer, and undermine the mucosa. At first the ulcers are small and separated by congested-appearing mucosa. As the tunneling continues, the small ulcers coalesce and form large ones with ragged, undermined edges. Scrapings from the bases of these ulcers on proctoscopy may reveal the organisms and are diagnostic, as is histologic study of biopsy specimens.

Fulminating amebic colitis is a lethal complication and may be likened to toxic megacolon. It isn't common but is to be suspected when a patient has severe, bloody, mucoid diarrhea, electrolyte loss, and signs of impending or actual colonic perforation with peritonitis. Fulminating amebic colitis requires prompt surgical intervention. Although the case described here was not one of fulminating generalized colitis, perforation of the cecum had occurred, creating the signs and symptoms of appendicitis and peritonitis. Surgery was mandatory, as it would be in fulminating colitis wherein sloughing of the mucosa occurs with the likelihood of multiple perforations. Subtotal colectomy with ileostomy or colostomy must be performed as a lifesaving measure, with medical therapy quickly added.

Not only did this patient have the rare condition of an amebic granuloma, so-called ameboma, of the cecum, but that organ had also become so inflamed as to create a localized peritonitis and then also perforated. Such a chain of events has been known to occur, although rarely.[10] The muscular coat of the colon is relatively resistant to this type of infestation, but it and the serosa may be penetrated, with resulting perforation and peritonitis as occurred in this patient. Tumor-like masses of granulomatous tissue that formed as part of the fibroblastic response to repeated amebic invasion did not contain the diagnostic organisms. The entire specimen simulated carcinoma.

Surgical intervention in patients with amebic colitis is said to carry a high mortality rate,[2] especially if the disease is not or cannot be recognized. In the clinically silent, insidious form of this disease, however, whose first presenting sign is, as in this patient, a complication that requires surgery, the clinician cannot possibly be held to classical tenets of treatment.

Unfortunately, this patient's amebic liver abscess wasn't noticed at the first operation. Its perforation with resulting overwhelming peritonitis led to her death. With hindsight, the chest X-ray, which preoperatively showed a possibly elevated right diaphragm, becomes meaningful. When the pathologist ruled out cancer and couldn't find evidence of a "specific granulomatous inflammation," perhaps serologic tests, indirect hemagglutination, complement fixation, or gel diffusion precipitation would have aided in making an earlier diagnosis postoperatively and clarified the intra-abdominal and/or hepatic picture.

It's well known that an amebic liver abscess can represent acute disease of less than a week's duration or may be present for several months. Amebic liver abscess is always secondary to intestinal amebiasis, although often the diagnosis has to be made without evidence of the primary luminal disease.[5] Such was the situation with this patient. Rosoff[5] stated that it is unusual to have coexisting amebic dysentery in its usual connotation, and that even diarrhea is not frequently encountered concurrently or by history. Cysts or trophozoites are demonstrated in the stools in fewer than 15 per cent of patients with liver abscess.

In 1935 Ochsner and DeBakey[11, 12] laid down three guiding principles of treatment of amebic liver abscess that are as valid today as they were then. It remains moot whether those principles could have been readily applied in this case or, if applied, would have resulted in a favorable outcome. Nonetheless, not to recognize or to overlook the possibility of amebic infestation in a nonendemic area can result in most unfortunate consequences.[14]

References

1. Pontes JF: Digestive system. Part II. Lower digestive tract. In *The Ciba Collection of Medical Illustrations* (Netter FH, ed), vol 3, section XII, plate 42, p 156. Summit, NJ: Ciba, 1975
2. Cohn I, Nance FC: Amebic colitis. In *Davis-Christopher Textbook of Surgery* (Sabiston DC, ed), 11th ed, p 1097. Philadelphia: Saunders, 1977
3. Powell SJ: Latest developments in the treatment of amebiasis. *Adv Pharmacol Chemother* 10:91, 1972
4. Goldsmith RS: Infectious diseases: Protozoal. In *Current Medical Diagnosis and Treatment* (Krupp MA, Chatton MJ, eds), 16th ann rev. p 841. Los Altos, Calif: Lange, 1977
5. Rosoff L: Amebic abscess of the liver. In *Davis-Christopher Textbook of Surgery* (Sabiston DC, ed), 11th ed, p 1214. Philadelphia: Saunders, 1977
6. Mahmoud AAF: Amebiasis. *Curr Ther*, p 2, 1975
7. Nair KG, Kothari NN, Sheth UK: Intravenous metronidazole in amoebic liver abscess. *Lancet* 1:1238, 1974
8. Craig CF, Faust EC: *Clinical Parasitology*. Philadelphia: Lea & Febiger, 1955
9. McHardy GG, et al: Panel: Intestinal infestations. In *Proceedings of the World Congress of Gastroenterology (Washington, 1958)*, vol 2, p 774. Baltimore: Williams & Wilkins, 1959
10. Stitt ER, Clough PW, Clough MC: *Practical Bacteriology, Haematology and Animal Parasitology*, pp 406-417. Philadelphia: Blakiston, 1938
11. Rives JD, Heibner WC, Powell JL: The surgical complications of amebiasis of the colon (exclusive of liver abscess). *Surg Clin North Am* 45:1421, 1965
12. Ochsner A, DeBakey M: Amebic hepatitis and hepatic abscess. *Surgery* 13:460, 612, 1943
13. Ochsner A, DeBakey M: Diagnosis and treatment of amebic abscess of the liver. *Am J Dig Dis* 2:47, 1935
14. Parks AG, Thomson PS: Rectum and anal canal. In *Davis-Christopher Textbook of Surgery* (Sabiston DC, ed), 11th ed, p 1140. Philadelphia: Saunders, 1977

36

Splenic rupture and infectious mononucleosis

An 18-year-old woman complained to her family physician of generalized malaise, easy fatigability, a sore throat, and a headache of eight days' duration. She had no chest pain, abdominal pain, or cough, but had experienced an occasional bout of nausea with some vomiting. When she was first seen, her temperature was 101°F. She had a thin, grayish-white, exudative tonsillitis, and her uvula and palatal arch appeared glassy, gelatinous, and edematous.

The cervical lymph nodes were enlarged (so-called anterior and posterior chains), but there was no other adenopathy. There was some mild abdominal distress in the left upper quadrant, described more specifically as a peculiar sensation when the patient turned or rolled over in bed. Neither the spleen nor the liver edge was palpable. No erythematous maculopapular skin eruption on the trunk or extremities was seen, nor was there any supraorbital edema. There was no clinical jaundice.

Laboratory studies revealed increased lymphocytes and monocytes in the peripheral blood smear, with 20 per cent atypical forms. The white blood count was slightly over 12,000. The platelet count was within normal limits. There was no anemia. A heterophil antibody titer was diagnostic of infectious mononucleosis. Other laboratory tests showed minimal to mild increases in serum glutamic-oxaloacetic transaminase, alkaline phosphatase, and bilirubin. The patient was admitted to the hospital.

Therapy was symptomatic: bed rest, stool softeners, salicylates, gargling and warm saline throat irrigations, intravenous distilled water and glucose, and observation. There was little change over the next three days. On the morning of the fourth day after hospital admission, while at stool, the patient suddenly felt faint and dizzy, "like blacking out," and when back in bed complained of severe pain in the abdomen, more generalized than localized to any one region. She vomited. At this time the vital signs showed a blood pressure of 116/68, pulse 96, and respirations 24.

The abdominal pain became more severe, and the patient fainter and paler. Three hours after the initial onset of abdominal pain, her blood pressure had fallen to 86/48 and her pulse rate was 110. An hour later abdominal pain was still present; the patient was cool and diaphoretic, with blood pressure 78/30 and pulse 136, and in shock. The attending physician was now at the bedside; emergency measures were employed, but the patient remained in shock. It appeared irreversible. She was rushed to the operating room with a diagnosis of spontaneous rupture of the spleen.

At surgery free blood was present in the abdominal cavity. The spleen had indeed ruptured. It was removed, but despite all resuscitative measures the patient died.

At autopsy the spleen contained a large subcapsular hematoma with an irregular perforation-laceration along the lower surface. The capsule appeared completely stripped from the underlying parenchyma. The splenic architecture showed marked disruption and was soft and friable.

Microscopically the capsule was infiltrated with mononuclear cells, most of which appeared to be lymphocytes. This striking infiltration of the fibromuscular structure of splenic trabeculae and capsule by mononuclear cells, with complete replacement in areas, seemed to make rupture or capsular tear inevitable regardless of any limitation of physical activity (straining at stool?).

Suit was filed against the family physician, alleging failure to make a timely diagnosis of spontaneous splenic rupture that caused the patient to bleed to death.

Discussion and comment. Splenic rupture is the most common cause of death in patients with infectious mononucleosis but occurs in only 0.2 to 0.4 per cent of recognized cases of the disease.[1-4] Its rare incidence and occasionally undramatic symptomatology, which is difficult to differentiate from the customary signs and symptoms of infectious mononucleosis itself, can make it a formidable problem in diagnosis.[5, 6] Natural reluctance to perform major surgery on an already weakened patient compounds the problem, although time is of the essence.

The spleen is enlarged in 50 to 60 per cent of patients with infectious mononucleosis. Although it's notoriously vulnerable to rupture,[3] rupture seldom occurs. And in this patient, whose spleen had not enlarged, rupture would be unexpected indeed.

The majority of patients with infectious mononucleosis don't have complications, and a somewhat cavalier attitude surrounds the disease.[1, 2] According to Hoagland,[2] misconceptions of the complications of infectious mononucleosis (and their frequency) stem from a disregard for diagnostic criteria, from an understandable desire not to report confusing complications, and from impressions of subspecialists who usually don't see uncomplicated cases.

Whenever a patient experiences severe or even moderate pain below the left costal margin, the diagnosis of a ruptured spleen should be considered. The development of abdominal pain in the left upper quadrant is generally followed by diffuse abdominal pain or pain radiating to the left shoulder. Nausea, vomiting, tachycardia, abdominal distention, shifting dullness, and other signs indicative of an acute abdominal crisis will follow.[1, 2, 5] When faintness and weakness occur and are followed by signs of hypovolemia, there should be little doubt about the diagnosis.

This patient's pain was more generalized, without radiation to the left shoulder area and with little abdominal tenderness, distention, or muscle spasms. She did vomit, but had been doing so prior to the acute episode. The chief signs and symptoms of the patient following sudden appearance of abdominal pain were those suggesting blood loss. Tachycardia was prominent although its cause was not identified. But since abdominal complaints in patients with infectious mononucleosis are infrequent, one should entertain the possibility of splenic rupture when they do occur.

To draw a distinction between subcapsular hematoma formation and ensuing splenic rupture is clinically impracticable. Small rents in the capsule will occur just above the hematoma. They may seal over temporarily but reopen hours, even days, later, followed by an explosive rupture. Thus, as I've said, whenever a patient with infectious mononucleosis has left upper abdominal or left subcostal pain or even generalized abdominal pain, especially when it's accompanied by tachycardia, immediate surgical exploration is indicated, without waiting for further blood volume studies.

Infectious mononucleosis produces an almost violent proliferation of lymphoid elements within the spleen. Edema, infiltration, and erosion of the capsule and connective tissue trabeculae are prominent features. The red pulp rapidly enlarges and exerts pressure on the connective tissue trabeculae and capsule.[1, 2, 5] According to Carter and Penman,[1] "It is certainly striking that splenomegaly, hyperplasia of the red pulp, vascular engorgement, infiltration and erosion of the connective tissue framework, and thrombocytopenia are all maximal at two to three weeks after the onset of the illness—the time when splenic rupture is most common."

That spleens in such a tenuous condition will rupture is not surprising. It may happen while the patient is straining at stool, from frequent abdominal examinations, or even from rolling over in bed,[1, 2, 4, 5] but rupture can also occur spontaneously. This patient may have strained at stool, although she was given softeners. Rupture did occur on about the 12th day of disease, which is within the commonly described time interval when this life-endangering complication occurs (usually 10 to 21 days after the onset of illness) and might possibly have been spontaneous.

Approximately 20 per cent of splenic ruptures are fatal.[1] Thrombocytopenia, which occurs in almost 50 per cent of patients with infectious mononucleosis, has been reported in association with a ruptured spleen,[1] but aside from this the warning signals that might predict this dangerous complication are pitifully few. An enlarged spleen during the second or third week of illness could be another sign that might alert the physician. Although this patient's spleen did not feel enlarged, the "peculiar sensation" in her abdomen that she reported as early as the eighth day of disease suggests that some change had taken place. Certainly her physician's exposure resulted from failure to keep splenic rupture in mind.

References

1. Carter RL, Penman HG: *Infectious Mononucleosis*, pp 26, 37, 38, 152. Oxford: Blackwell, 1969
2. Hoagland RJ: *Infectious Mononucleosis*, pp 15, 61, 124. New York: Grune and Stratton, 1967
3. Infectious mononucleosis. In *Merck Manual of Diagnosis and Therapy* (Holvey DN, ed), 12th ed, pp 216, 331. Rahway, NJ: Merck Sharp & Dohme, 1972
4. Niederman JC: Infectious mononucleosis. In *Harrison's Principles of Internal Medicine*, 7th ed, p 1063. New York: McGraw-Hill, 1974
5. Hoagland RJ, Henson HM: Splenic rupture in infectious mononucleosis. *Ann Intern Med* 46:1184, 1957
6. Niederman JC, Evans AS, Subrahmanyan L, et al: Prevalence, incidence and persistence of EB virus antibody in young adults. *N Engl J Med* 282:361, 1970

37

Bilateral Wilms' tumors (nephroblastomas, embryomas of the kidney)

A 3-year-old boy was seen by his family physician for a running nose, mild fever, and sore throat. The mother described what could best be called malaise, but there was no abdominal pain or cramps. The history seemed typical of an upper respiratory infection.

Examination revealed a reddened, injected pharynx, inflamed tonsils without suppuration, some rhinitis, and shotty, slightly enlarged cervical lymph nodes. The chest was clear, heart sounds unremarkable, and blood pressure normal. The abdomen was slightly protuberant and rounded, but soft and not tender. No masses were felt. The liver, spleen, and kidneys were not palpable. There were no hernias, umbilical or inguinal. The child recovered uneventfully on supportive care.

He was seen again on two different occasions, about a month apart. Each examination revealed only mild pharyngitis and tonsillitis. The abdomen was examined by palpation alone; each time, although it remained rounded and protuberant, no masses were felt and there were no abdominal complaints.

Approximately four or five months after the initial visit, the same physician was called early in the morning because of upper abdominal pain. The child was seen immediately. On examination he was in no acute distress but appeared pale. He had a fever of 101°F. The abdomen was still protuberant but not tender. Large masses of about 12 cm were felt over each kidney (flank) area. The patient was admitted to the hospital.

Laboratory studies revealed mild anemia and a normal white blood count. The urinalysis was unremarkable. There was no hematuria. Abdominal X-rays showed bilateral masses overlying the kidney areas, with no calcification. Intravenous pyelograms showed the kidney pelves and calices stretched out over the tumors, which were situated in the superior half of each kidney. The tumors did not displace or obstruct the calices or kidney pelves. Each kidney was functioning. The picture was deemed characteristic of bilateral Wilms' tumors. A chest X-ray was negative for metastasis. Abdominal surgery was performed without further studies other than routine general preoperative care.

Surgery showed extensive involvement of each kidney by large tumors. They were not multinodular but were each made up of a single, large nodule that had not perforated or ruptured. On microscopic analysis the tumors proved to be Wilms' tumors (nephroblastomas). They were felt to be histologically aggressive because they were composed for the most part of small undifferentiated cells that were arranged in large, solid sheets without an epithelial component.[1]

The tumors extended outward and downward into the perirenal fat pads and toward each kidney pedicle. On the right side, tumor involvement extended almost to the lower third of the kidney; on the left, to beyond the inferior half. In spite of their size, the tumors were lying relatively free without involvement of the liver, diaphragm, spleen, adjacent pancreas, or a loop of intestine. Enlarged renal and periaortic lymph nodes indicative of metastases were present, but the vena cava and aorta were not involved. "Early" renal vein infiltration was present on each side.

Total resection of the tumors was accomplished, including the regional lymph nodes in the renal and periaortic areas. Partial nephrectomies were performed, leaving one-third of the kidney on the right and slightly less than half on the left. The patient withstood the procedure surprisingly well, without sustaining a leak from the pelvis or remaining parenchyma of either kidney. Postoperative radiation therapy, 2,000 rads, was given to each renal tumor bed, followed by chemotherapy.

The patient had remained free of disease for almost 10 months at the time his case was studied. Nonetheless, suit was filed against the family physician, alleging failure to make a prompt diagnosis of an intra-abdominal cancer.

Discussion and comment. The tumor is named for the Germân surgeon Max Wilms, who described it in 1899,[2] and a classical description appears in *Holt's Diseases of Infancy and Childhood*, circa 1930.[3] It's worth repeating:

> Arising from fetal rests, [the tumors] may contain different types of tissue exhibiting various degrees of differentiation, and may vary in their rate of growth. As a rule they develop in the first five years of life. In Wollstein's [*Arch Pathol Lab Med* 3:1, 1927] series more than

a third were recognized in the first year. Boys and girls are about equally affected, and these tumors arise equally often on the left or right side. At first surrounded by a fibrous capsule, the tumor tends eventually to break through this boundary, so that finally the whole kidney may be infiltrated as well as other contiguous structures. It may grow from any part of the kidney and may distort it in various ways. Many of these tumors are hard; others are soft and vascular. The consistency is rarely uniform throughout, and even the firmest mass may contain fluctuant areas of necrosis or hemorrhage. Metastasis to the lungs occurs late and may be lacking in some of the cases, but invariably the malignant character expresses itself in infiltration and direct extension. By invasion of the renal vein the tumor has been known to extend by continuous growth as far as the heart. Pressure symptoms may arise because of the tumor's relation to the diaphragm, the digestive tract, the urinary tract, or the great veins.

In the majority of cases no symptoms are noticeable until the tumor is palpated. Its presence is often discovered by the parents but only after it has reached considerable size. Local pain and hematuria sometimes attract early attention. As a rule, anemia, cachexia, and pressure symptoms giving rise to dyspnea, severe constipation, frequent urination, or edema appear relatively late. At first resembling simply an enlarged kidney, the mass grows forward and downward, losing its mobility as it infiltrates and becomes attached to the parietes and to other organs. Tumors arising in the left kidney are often mistaken for an enlarged spleen. Differentiation from cystic kidney or hydronephrosis is sometimes more difficult. Pyelography usually shows encroachment by the mass on some part of the renal pelvis. Although gross hematuria is rare, microscopic blood appears from time to time at irregular intervals.

The published incidence of Wilms' tumor varies from 15 to 40 per cent of solid tumors occurring in childhood.[4] Reported series would naturally show this variation, and it shouldn't be considered unusual. Current methods of treatment have dramatically improved the survival rate over the past decade or two,[1, 4-10] to the point where Wilms' tumors now carry probably the best prognosis of all intra-abdominal neoplasms in children.[4] The two-year survival rate of patients with Wilms' tumor has risen from about 50 per cent a few decades ago to 80 per cent.[4, 7-9, 11] Despite this astounding progress, individual prognoses must take into account factors such as bilaterality, tumor size, number of tumor nodules, rupture, adhesions, regional lymph node involvement, renal vein infiltration, and epithelial differentiation.[1]

Without question, the treatment of choice for Wilms' tumor is the triad of surgical resection of all or as much of the tumor as possible, postoperative radiation therapy, and chemotherapy. This triad has made all the difference in prognosis.[4, 6, 10, 12, 13] Before surgery is performed all reasonable diagnostic measures should be employed, but the patient need not be studied to death. These measures may include cystoscopy, retrograde pyelograms, renal scans, ultrasonic scans, arteriography (especially helpful to rule out bilateral tumors), and inferior vena cavograms.

An intravenous pyelogram is the backbone of the diagnostic work-up. It will often show the characteristic findings of Wilms' tumor: distortion of the pelves and calices as they're stretched out over the tumor, rather than displacement or obstruction from an extra renal mass.[4] The majority of Wilms' tumors do not destroy renal function. A chest X-ray is mandatory to rule out the most likely distant metastases; perhaps as many as 50 per cent of patients will have pulmonary involvement when first seen.[4]

Hypertension is an occasional accompanying symptom, but the initial sign of disease is an abdominal mass felt by parent or physician. Unfortunately, abdominal examination of an uncooperative or apprehensive child is hardly a sensitive diagnostic test. The deep-lying, well-protected kidneys prevent a renal tumor from becoming palpable until it reaches a certain size. Until symptoms occur or a palpable size is reached, these tumors simply defy detection. Early diagnosis is understandably a matter of luck.

Bilateral Wilms' tumors, of which this case is an example, occur in 5 to 10 per cent of cases.[4, 10, 14-17] The similarities to unilateral disease are obvious, but there are distinct differences and patients with bilateral tumors should be studied separately.[1] The clinical difficulties naturally are doubled. It isn't known whether the two tumors develop independently and simultaneously or whether one spreads to the other kidney. Since multiple sites of origin are seen in unilateral tumors, it's reasonable to assume that bilateral Wilms' tumors represent independent growths. Most often they appear simultaneously. Occasionally they may be separated by months or even years.[15] Bilateral tumors are usually seen in a younger age group than unilateral tumors.[14-18]

Bilateral Wilms' tumors have a different mutational pattern

from unilateral tumors.[14, 15, 18] Bilateral tumor initiation follows two specific patterns. One mutation may be inherited; the other occurs in a somatic cell and converts it to a tumor cell. Hereditary tumors are acquired earlier than nonhereditary tumors and are more likely to be bilateral.[18] Unfortunately, it isn't yet possible to identify which parents will have offspring at risk, except that all bilateral cases should be presumed to be of the hereditary type.[18]

Patients with simultaneous, multifocal, bilateral Wilms' tumors are different clinically from those who have a unifocal tumor in one kidney and later develop a second unifocal tumor in the other. There's a much higher incidence of associated congenital anomalies than in patients with unilateral disease.[14-18] Reported anomalies include bilateral aniridia, horseshoe kidneys, duplication of the upper urinary tract, aplastic and/or hypoplastic kidneys, and, in males, hypospadias and cryptorchidism. Children with bilateral disease are frequently born of mothers older than average, and their age at diagnosis is lower than average for Wilms' tumor patients in general.[15]

Initial treatment of bilateral Wilms' tumors by surgery requires modification, compromise, innovation, and judgment. No one plan can be considered standard procedure. Open biopsy, followed by radiation therapy and then extensive resection, and initial resection and postoperative radiation both have their place. The triad of surgery, radiation, and chemotherapy, however, yields the highest survival figures, including patients with lung metastases.

Radical surgical excision, including all node-bearing metastases, may be the most important factor in the treatment of Wilms' tumor. Yet it may not be feasible or even necessary in cases of bilateral disease. In these patients partial nephrectomies—so-called shelling out of the tumors—is practiced. It may be followed by radiation therapy and chemotherapy and later by a second-look operation to remove residual disease. Variations and combinations of treatment programs in this disease are protean.

Radiation dosages, understandably, should be kept within the lowest tumoricidal range. Hussey et al[19] have reported that a postoperative dose as low as 2,000 rads is sufficient. Others feel even 1,800 rads may do the job.[4] Anticancer drugs are given in maintenance dosages for prolonged periods.[6]

Eventually it might become mandatory to remove all remaining kidney tissue, whether because of chronic renal failure due to radiation therapy or chemotherapy or because of recurrent cancer. Renal transplantation would be the natural recourse in such an instance.[16] It also appears to be a logical choice in the treatment of bilateral Wilms' tumors when the more conventional avenues can't be followed.[16, 19]

The physician in this case could hardly be faulted for failing to diagnose "an intra-abdominal cancer" when the tumors weren't large enough to be felt on careful palpation. Surgery was performed without delay, and the patient's prognosis appeared favorable. Exposure would seem to be based mostly on parental concern, which, though understandable, has little basis in clinical reality.

References

1. Lemerle J, Tournade MF, Marchant RG, et al: Wilms' tumor: Natural history and prognostic factors. *Cancer* 37:2557, 1976
2. Wilms M: *Die Mischgeschwülste der Niere*. Leipsig: Georgi, 1899
3. Holt LE, McIntosh R: *Holt's Diseases of Infancy and Childhood,* 11th ed, p 843. New York: Appleton-Century, 1936
4. Holder TM, Leape LL: Pediatric surgery. In *Davis-Christopher Textbook of Surgery* (Sabiston DC, ed), 11th ed, pp 1389-1391. Philadelphia: Saunders, 1977
5. Aron BS: Wilms' tumor. A clinical study of eighty-one patients. *Cancer* 33:637, 1974
6. Bodey GP, Frei E III: Medical therapy of cancer. In *Harrison's Principles of Internal Medicine,* 7th ed, pp 1690, 1694, 1697. New York: McGraw-Hill, 1974
7. D'Angio GJ: Management of children with Wilms' tumor. *Cancer* 30:1528, 1972
8. Grayhack JT: The urinary system. In *Davis-Christopher Textbook of Surgery* (Sabiston DC, ed), 11th ed, pp 1738, 1739. Philadelphia: Saunders, 1977
9. Hussey DH, Castro JR, Sullivan MP, et al: Radiation therapy in management of Wilms' tumor. *Radiology* 101:663, 1971
10. Lytton B, Epstein FH: Tumors of the urinary tract. In *Harrison's Principles of Internal Medicine,* 7th ed, p 1415. New York: McGraw-Hill, 1974
11. Graham JB: Renal malignancies. In *Urologic Surgery* (Glenn JF, ed), 2nd ed, p 73. New York: Harper & Row, 1975
12. Farber S: Chemotherapy in the treatment of leukemia and Wilms' tumor. *JAMA* 198:154, 1966
13. Holland JF, Frei E III (eds): *Cancer Medicine*. Philadelphia: Lea & Febiger, 1973
14. Bond JV: Bilateral Wilms' tumour and urinary-tract anomalies. *Lancet* 2:721, 1975
15. Bond JV: Bilateral Wilms' tumour. Age at diagnosis, associated congenital anomalies, and possible pattern of inheritance. *Lancet* 2:482, 1975
16. Ehrlich RM, Goldman R, Kaufman JJ: Surgery of bilateral Wilms' tumors: The role of renal transplantation. *J Urol* 111:277, 1974
17. Fay R, Brosman S, Williams DI: Bilateral nephroblastoma. *J Urol* 110:119, 1973
18. Knudson AG, Strong LC: Mutation and cancer: A model for Wilms' tumor of the kidney. *J Natl Cancer Inst* 48:1029, 1972
19. DeLorimier AA, Belzer FO, Kountz SL, et al: Treatment of bilateral Wilms' tumor. *Am J Surg* 122:275, 1971

38

Endometriosis and ovarian cancer

A 32-year-old woman, gravida 1, para 1, was referred to a board-certified gynecologist because of abdominal cramps, repetitive menstrual pain, and generalized abdominal discomfort. A clinical diagnosis of endometriosis was made. The patient's mother and one maternal aunt had had uterine cancer, but there was no family history of endometriosis. Examination was consistent with ovarian and uterine signs of endometriosis. Each ovary felt slightly enlarged and tender, as did the uterine fundus. The pelvic organs were not easily mobile, and there was the suggestion of tender cul-de-sac nodulations. The patient had been carefully observed by a previous physician, managed medically, and become pregnant, but was relieved only slightly following delivery.

Symptoms continued, and because of increasing abdominal pain surgery was advised. At laparotomy intense adhesions with some chocolate-filled cysts were found binding down the left tube and ovary. The right tube and ovary were also involved with adhesions, but to a lesser degree. The uterus was thought to be enlarged. Small endometriomas were present in the cul-de-sac. A total hysterectomy, left salpingo-oophorectomy, resection of endometriomas, and incidental appendectomy were performed. The right ovary appeared to be normal and was left in place; the right tube was removed. The pathology report did not confirm the diagnosis of endometriosis, but the tissue removed was friable and necrotic. No specific histologic diagnosis was made, but the patient's symptoms were relieved.

Two years later she began to experience abdominal discomfort with some bloating. Abdominal cramping became severe. Pelvic examination revealed fullness in the cul-de-sac. Operation was advised.

At surgery generalized abdominal carcinomatosis was found.

The right ovary was totally replaced by a papillary serous cystadenocarcinoma; omental and peritoneal implants showed an identical histology.

Despite all supportive measures and chemotherapy, the patient died five months later at the age of 35. Suit was filed against the gynecologist, alleging failure to prevent ovarian cancer by not removing both ovaries prophylactically and also as a therapeutic measure in the treatment of endometriosis.

Discussion and comment. Despite the lack of histologic evidence of endometriosis following the first operation, it was a reasonable presumptive diagnosis. Novak, Jones, and Jones[1] had this to say regarding histologic verification of endometriosis:

> Because of the constant recurrence of menstrual desquamation with perhaps the pressure of the retained menstrual blood in the cyst cavities, the endometrial lining of the latter may be almost completely absent and in its place one may see only reactive connective tissue elements, with usually a large number of endothelial leukocytes heavily laden with blood pigment (pseudoxanthoma cells). Indeed, in about one-third of all cases of typical even extensive clinical endometriosis as seen at operation there may be no histological proof of its existence, even if many pathological sections are made.

The patient's prior medical management resulted in pregnancy and certainly cannot be criticized. Treatment was individualized for the patient.[2-4] When it failed to relieve her symptoms, surgery was the only reasonable alternative because of the potentially destructive nature of the pathologic process and its erratic pattern of progression. Acute complications of the disease—for example, rupture of ovarian endometriomas—become emergencies and account for 5 to 10 per cent of surgical operations for endometriosis.[1, 3] In these situations the need for surgery is indisputable.

When there's no emergency, conservative surgery is the treatment of choice in younger women. There's often good reason to resect endometriosis and, if possible, retain reproductive function in young women who wish to conceive, because approximately 60 per cent of these patients will conceive within one month to two years postoperatively.[3,5] The extent of surgery will depend to some degree on the amount and distribution of the disease. Symptoms don't always correlate with the severity of the disease. A small endometrioma, for example, may impinge on more nerve endings than a large one.[3] In women past the childbearing years, total hysterectomy and bilateral salpingo-oophorectomy are preferable.[6]

Conservative surgery is often called for in patients known to have single large endometriomas or extensive adnexal adhesions. That implies minimal resection, removing as much of the endometriosis as possible but conserving tissue necessary for reproduction. In this patient neither a conservative nor a radical approach would have been acceptable. Her surgery was individualized.

The malpractice exposure here lies in the development of cancer in the remaining ovary, which at the first operation appeared normal but subsequently became cancerous.[6, 7] It's always been debatable whether to remove both normal ovaries in a woman between 30 and 35 when surgery is performed for a benign condition.[8-10] The endometriosis compounds the dilemma in this patient.

One school of thought recommends that, because ovarian cancer has a very poor prognosis, both ovaries should be removed prophylactically in a woman in this age group if she has decided that she wishes no more children. A far more popular, less radical point of view is the one illustrated by this case. In a woman under 35, perhaps even 40, every effort should be made to maintain normal ovarian function by leaving one or at least part of one ovary in place. That's the prevailing opinion among most general and gynecologic surgeons, and it's well supported in medical circles.[11-13]

Was the occurrence of cancer in this patient's remaining ovary coincidental—or was the cancer overlooked in the first place? Ranney[3] reported that four of his patients with endometriosis had endometrioid adenocarcinomas of the ovary, but he didn't mention a papillary serous cystadenocarcinoma. There's no way of knowing whether a cancer was missed in this patient at the first operation. The pathology report on the left ovary and total uterus, removed at that operation, was nondescript.

The interval of two years and a few months between operations would fit the usual progression of an ovarian cancer of the type reported, which, untreated, could resemble what was found at the second operation. The development of ovarian cancer is made more complex by the patient's family history of uterine cancer. Although there's no established hereditary relationship between the two, the lay patient tends to think there is, creating exposure for the physician, no matter how unwarranted. But if a hereditary factor were proved, would it be an indication for removal of what appears to be a normal ovary from a 32-year-old woman? One would think not, although the question can and should be debated.

References

1. Novak ER, Jones GS, Jones HW Jr: *Novak's Textbook of Gynecology*, 9th ed, p 548. Baltimore: Williams & Wilkins, 1975
2. Chalmers JA: Medical management of endometriosis. *Br Med J* 1(6075):1532, 1977
3. Ranney B: The prevention, inhibition, palliation, and treatment of endometriosis. *Am J Obstet Gynecol* 123:778, 1975
4. Sadigh H, Naples JD Jr, Batt RE: Conservative surgery for endometriosis in the infertile couple. *Obstet Gynecol* 49:562, 1977
5. Devereaux WP: Endometriosis: Long term observations with particular reference to the incidence of pregnancy. *Obstet Gynecol* 22:444, 1963
6. Finsterwalder E, Wagner-Kolb D: The problem of ovarian cancer after preceding gynecological operations. Case report with special reference to endometriosis. *Geburtshilfe Frauenheilkd* 35:783, 1975
7. Dockerty MB: Malignancy complicating endometriosis. *Am J Obstet Gynecol* 83:175, 1962
8. Decker DG, Mussey E, Williams TJ, et al: Grading of gynecologic malignancy; epithelial ovarian cancer. In *Proceedings of the Seventh National Cancer Conference*, pp 223-231. Philadelphia: Lippincott, 1973
9. Williams TJ, Symmonds RE, Litwak O: Management of unilateral and encapsulated ovarian cancer in young women. *Gynecol Oncol* 1:143, 1973
10. Williams TJ, Dockerty MB: Status of the contralateral ovary in encapsulated low grade malignant tumors of the ovary. *Surg Gynecol Obstet* 143:763, 1976
11. Aure JC, Hoeg K, Kolstad P: Clinical and histologic studies of ovarian carcinoma. Long-term follow-up of 990 cases. *Obstet Gynecol* 37:1, 1971
12. Bagley CM, Young RC, Canellos GP, et al: Treatment of ovarian carcinoma: Possibilities for progress. *N Engl J Med* 287:856, 1972
13. Clark DGC, Hilaris BS, Ochoa M Jr, et al: Interdisciplinary approach to advanced ovarian cancer. *Surg Clin North Am* 54:897, 1974

Section III

Selected clinical problems

The five cases that form this section were selected to illustrate specific problems that don't fit neatly into the anatomic categories of Section II. Some of these problems are relatively rare and therefore present diagnostic as well as therapeutic challenges.

Like the case studies in Section II, each of the following histories is followed by a discussion that emphasizes the clinical basis of malpractice exposure.

39

Obturator hernia: Inguinal hernia and postoperative pain

A 63-year-old woman was referred to a board-certified general surgeon because of vague pain in the general area of the right lower quadrant of the abdomen and the right groin. The pain radiated downward along the inner side of her right thigh to the knee. No other signs and symptoms were present, and a systemic review was negative. The discomfort had been present for about five or six days.

On examination there was nothing to suggest an intra-abdominal problem, and no obvious hernia was felt within the inguinal or femoral canals. The patient had no urinary complaints, and a rectal examination was unremarkable. The only possible finding that could be elicited was the faintest suggestion of a vague, soft, nontender 2- by 2.5-cm lump in the midportion of the right inguinal canal. She was re-examined 48 hours later and had little change in symptoms. The suggestion of a lump in the right inguinal canal was no longer present.

A presumptive diagnosis of an inguinal hernia or a hernia of the obturator canal was made. At exploration the obturator foramen was examined in the preperitoneal space. It was visualized through an abdominal preperitoneal approach.[1] The inguinal ligament was surgically divided just medial to its insertion on the anterior iliac spine and reflected medially with the above-lying abdominal musculature and fascia, and the tissues were then separated gently down to the obturator canal. No hernia was found, nor was a retroperitoneal tumor present. The inguinal ligament was reapproximated to the fibrous tissue along the medial aspect of the anterior iliac spine.

The femoral canal was within easy access through the single groin incision and it, too, showed no hernia. On exploration of the inguinal canal an indirect hernia was found, its sac ligated, and an uneventful repair accomplished.

Immediately postoperatively the patient complained of severe pain over the anterolateral aspect of her right thigh, along the course of the lateral femoral cutaneous nerve. She also complained of pain and numbness over the lower region of the inguinal canal near the pubic tubercle and over the extreme upper inner thigh and the right labia majora, all corresponding to the course of the ilioinguinal nerve and terminal branches of the genitofemoral nerve (external spermatic and lumboinguinal).[2]

Because of continued severe pain over the right lateral thigh, although the pain and numbness over the lower right groin had abated, the incision was re-explored one week later in the area medial and deep to the anterior iliac spine, where the lateral femoral cutaneous nerve courses in close approximation. The nerve, which is purely sensory, was found and described as lying easily in its bed without kinking or twisting and without trauma by suture. Nonetheless, because its normal course would run directly through the lateral extremity of the incision, it was purposely divided deep in the retroperitoneal area and its end secured with a neurosurgical clip. Postoperatively the patient complained of numbness and paresthesia without pain over the right anterolateral thigh. She also complained of continued slight paresthesia and pain in the extreme upper inner thigh, lower groin, and labia.

Eight months later, although the patient no longer had any complaints referable to the lateral thigh, she still had pain and paresthesia in the right labia and the upper inner thigh and groin. Surgical exploration of the inguinal canal was performed in hopes of finding a nerve end neuroma. None was found. Pain was only partly relieved after this procedure. Suit was filed against the surgeon alleging incompetent and careless surgery resulting in postoperative pain and leaving a foreign body, the neurosurgical clip, within the operative area.

Discussion and comment. Neurological complications following inguinal herniorrhaphy are not infrequent, and this case illustrates what can be a vexing problem.[1, 3] The ilioinguinal nerve, which is the principal nerve structure of concern, is often inadvertently traumatized, not necessarily by the surgeon. Injury to this nerve neither is life-threatening nor causes significant motor impairment, yet it can result in painful and annoying sequelae. Branches of the genitofemoral nerve also may be involved.

In a female the resulting numbness and paresthesias about the labia become psychologically annoying in addition to the painful stimuli about the groin and inner thigh. The occurrence of these symptoms with a bilateral inguinal hernia repair is, of course, doubly annoying. Although such postoperative symptoms usually disappear, even when they persist they can be considered an acceptable aftermath of hernia surgery, especially when all precautions are taken to avoid injuring the ilioinguinal nerve. Unfortunately, not all hernia repairs are simple; technical difficulties exist, and patients' individual threshholds to discomfort vary. Malpractice exposure isn't surprising.

This patient's preoperative signs were puzzling. The surgeon had to decide whether to trust in luck that a simple explanation—an inguinal hernia—would account for all her symptoms or to be thorough, examine the obturator space, and explore all possible causes. He chose the latter course.

There are numerous approaches to the retroperitoneal and obturator space.[4, 5] Releasing the inguinal ligament at its lateral attachment to the anterior iliac spine poses the risk of trauma to the lateral femoral cutaneous nerve, which courses just a few centimeters medial and deep to this structure. In addition, slightly medial to the anterior iliac spine the ilioinguinal nerve perforates the internal oblique muscle, from which it courses downward and medially through the inguinal canal. Both these nerves, therefore, are vulnerable to injury when the lateral extent of an incision approaches the region of the anterior iliac spine. When a retractor is placed within the incision and against the inner or medial portion of the anterior iliac spine, traction on it will inadvertently traumatize either or both nerves at this point.[2] Since both nerves course relatively close to each other in this specific area, they're equally exposed to traumatic neuritis produced by an overzealous or unwary assistant's pulling laterally on the retractor.

The vulnerability of the ilioinguinal and lateral femoral cutaneous nerves is one of the disadvantages of gaining access to the pre- and/or retroperitoneal space when the inguinal ligament is divided at the anterior spine. This space can be approached easily through a diagonal incision just above the ligament, with downward separation of the musculofascial layers, or by direct division of the inguinal ligament at its midportion in a region medial to the femoral nerve.

If the retractor is placed more deeply to expose the retroperitoneal structures and the obturator space, there's even more danger of trauma to these nerves as they emerge from the lumbar plexus: the ilioinguinal from the first lumbar root, the lateral femoral cutaneous from the second and third lumbar roots. They emerge at the lateral border of the psoas muscle and run gently downward and laterally toward the inner crest of the ilium, medial and deep to the anterior iliac spine. The tip of a deeply placed retractor that impinges on these nerves where they emerge from the musculature immediately overlying the lumbar plexus will cause painful sequelae over the courses of both nerves, and occasionally over the course of the genitofemoral nerve as well (external spermatic and lumboinguinal branches).[2] This complication is not infrequently seen following gynecologic operations, where it is necessary to obtain adequate exposure by placing retractors against the deeper tissues.[6]

This patient's traumatic neuritis was probably caused by placement of retractors within the incision near the anterior iliac spine to gain exposure. Lateral traction would thus cause trauma to the nerves in this vulnerable location.

An obturator hernia is often termed a hidden hernia, and its diagnosis is difficult. Possibly more suits could be filed alleging oversight of this type of hernia than are filed because of the symptoms of ilioinguinal and genitofemoral neuritis. A diagnostic feature of obturator hernia is pain that passes down the inner side of the thigh to the knee and corresponds to the radiation of the obturator nerve, the Howship-Romberg sign.[1, 4, 5] It was mentioned in this patient's history and symptom review. The patient also belonged to a group in whom obturator hernias are known to occur: elderly, female, and frail. The decision to explore the obturator space was sound in spite of a negative rectal examination. As a rule, only incarcerated or strangulated hernias in this area may be felt on rectal examination.[1, 4]

This case illustrates the intricacies of diagnosis and technical surgery in an area that's usually considered simple but can be quite complex. Resulting damage of the type that occurred here was minimal and is usually considered an acceptable concomitant of thorough, well-planned surgery. The neurosurgical clip can be discounted, since this is a highly approved and wholly acceptable method of managing a nerve end.

References

1. Nyhus LM, Bombeck CT: Hernias. In *Davis-Christopher Textbook of Surgery* (Sabiston DC, ed), 11th ed, pp 1347, 1355. Philadelphia: Saunders, 1977
2. *Morris' Human Anatomy*, 9th ed, pp 1078-1083. Philadephia: Blakiston, 1933
3. Moosman DA, Oelrich TM: Prevention of accidental trauma to the ilioinguinal nerve during inguinal herniorrhaphy. *Am J Surg* 133:146, 1977
4. Rogers FA: Strangulated obturator hernia. In *Hernia* (Nyhus LM, Harkins HN, eds), Philadelphia: Lippincott, 1964
5. Wakely CPG: Obturator hernia. *Br J Surg* 26:515, 1939
6. TeLinde RW, Mattingly RF: *Operative Gynecology*, 4th ed, pp 756-757. Philadelphia: Lippincott, 1970

40

Mesenteric venous thrombosis and inguinal herniorrhaphy

A 53-year-old man went to the emergency department of his local hospital with a persistent lump in the left groin of 48 hours' duration. He stated that he'd had a left inguinal hernia for eight years but had rejected recommendations for its repair. The lump was at the site of the long-standing hernia and could not be reduced. A diagnosis of incarcerated left inguinal hernia was made, and the patient was taken to surgery within two hours.

At surgery a direct hernia was described with a "sac" containing large intestine, presumably sigmoid. It appeared healthy and viable. The sac was opened, its contents reduced, and the hernia repaired without event. In the postoperative recovery room the patient's temperature suddenly rose to 103°F. Chest X-ray revealed a pneumonitis that was felt to be typical of a pulmonary infarct. Over the next seven days the patient ran a stormy course because of pulmonary complications, presumably from pulmonary emboli of unclear origin. There was an accompanying paralytic ileus, but no localized signs of any other intra-abdominal problem.

The patient's temperature remained elevated at 103°F, as did his white blood count, at 13,000 with a slight shift to the left. Adequate antibiotic and supportive care was given. On the eighth postoperative day the patient experienced severe pain, with guarding, in the left lower quadrant. His white count increased to 18,000 and his temperature rose to 104°F. He looked toxic. Sonography suggested an abscess.

Reoperation on the 10th postoperative day revealed a large abscess in the left lower quadrant associated with a perforation of the sigmoid colon and multiple small perforations of the ileum, which was caught up in the abscessed mass. Mesenteric abscesses were also present between loops of the small intestine and in the subhepatic space, more to the left than the right. Despite small intestinal resection and anastomosis, transverse colostomy, and multiple drainages, the patient's course went steadily downhill and he died three weeks later. Suit, filed against the surgeon, alleged failure to diagnose postoperative peritonitis and intra-abdominal abscess formation with resulting death.

Discussion and comment. Simple explanations of the complications following left direct inguinal hernia repair may be reasonable but not wholly accurate. The possible cause of these complications is worthy of further study. The "sac" (the hernia was described as direct) might have been only a pseudosac, so that opening it would have compromised the sigmoid's viability, creating later necrosis and perforation. It's also possible that the bowel could have been inadvertently squeezed, pinched, or injured by a suture in closing the "sac." A portion of the sigmoid was very likely a part of the wall of the "sac," which would have increased the likelihood of its torsion or twisting. Certainly the underlying cause of death was perforation of the sigmoid colon with resultant abscess formation, incorporation of the ileum, and peritonitis. Delayed recognition of this finding is the allegation of the suit and the point of exposure for the physician.

These explanations, however, don't account for the entire chain of events. It's necessary to look at other considerations, no matter how conjectural they may be. First, this was not just a case of a simple inguinal hernia repair. No long-standing incarcerated hernia can be considered simple. Second, the patient had pulmonary emboli resulting in pulmonary infarction, and an attempt to explain this must be made. The sudden rise in temperature immediately after operation was very likely due to the first of numerous recurring attacks of pulmonary infarction.

The incarcerated hernia in which the sigmoid was caught could easily have created swelling, edema, and an overlying inflammatory reaction in the related mesenteric veins, reducing the blood flow and increasing hypercoagulability and endothelial damage (Virchow's triad).[1, 2] Such an environment would be ideal for the development of mesenteric venous thrombosis with resulting embolic lung phenomena. Furthermore, as the mesenteric thromboses enlarged and propagated, the damaged portion of the sigmoid would develop venous gangrene and inevitably arterial compromise as well. Ultimately, bowel necrosis and perforation would occur.

Such intestinal compromise may not be readily apparent, since venous gangrene usually develops more slowly and is less dramatic than arterial gangrene. That would explain the lack of postoperative clinical symptoms in this patient. Peritonitis from a sigmoid perforation probably wasn't diagnosed early because it didn't happen early.

Five to seven days after the operation would have been needed for this type of vascular compromise of the sigmoid wall to reach the point where perforation would occur.

Venous gangrene of the sigmoid not only fits the entire clinical picture but also would explain the pulmonary emboli that caused the patient's temperature to rise so dramatically in the postoperative recovery room. The venous system of the mesentery on the left side of the colon could well have been compromised during the 48 hours of hernia incarceration the patient experienced before seeking medical aid. Twisting of the vessels of the sigmoid mesentery caught up in the incarceration would further compromise the venous return from the sigmoid and help create a thrombosis. It's reasonable that the sigmoid within the hernial sac did appear normal at operation. The venous obstruction would have been in its early stages, and clearly defined bowel compromise would not have been apparent. The critical changes that caused the colon to perforate came later. The patient's history, signs, and symptoms seem to fit the rare pattern of mesenteric venous thrombosis, a condition that's often fatal and involves many areas of the gastrointestinal tract, including the pancreas.[1, 3]

If one were to place the onus for this tragic outcome anywhere, it would have to be at the feet of the patient himself. First, unless there's some overriding general medical reason, all hernias should be repaired; the patient refused. Second, he delayed 48 hours before consulting a physician about his incarcerated hernia. The complications that occurred in this case are rare but still pose vexing problems that not only defy solution but, unfortunately, enhance the physician's exposure to malpractice.

References

1. Ludbrook J, Jamieson GG: Disorders of systemic veins. In *Davis-Christopher Textbook of Surgery* (Sabiston DC, ed), 11th ed, pp 1827, 1830. Philadelphia: Saunders, 1977
2. Virchow RLK: *Thrombose und Embolie*. Leipzig: Barth, 1910
3. Hirsh J, Gallus AS: ^{125}I-labeled fibrinogen scanning: Use in the diagnosis of venous thrombosis. *JAMA* 233:970, 1975

41

Mesenteric artery atherosclerosis and intestinal infarction

A 52-year-old woman had one episode of a slightly bloody, loose stool accompanied by generalized upper abdominal pain and nausea. She vomited once during the episode and described a small amount of blood in the vomitus. Closer questioning revealed that the pain had been present for about five days; the bloody stool and vomitus were noted three days after the onset of pain. An upper gastrointestinal X-ray series suggested some stomach and duodenal deformity, possibly peptic ulcer.

The patient was admitted to the hospital for study and evaluation. She gave a history of abdominal discomfort off and on for the past year, with pain after eating and some bloating and indigestion. She stated that she frequently took antacids. A review of systems elicited nothing pertinent. She did not drink alcoholic beverages, and there was no history of abdominal trauma.

On examination she was not in acute distress but looked ill. The abdomen was slightly distended with some mild central tenderness. No masses were felt. There was no stool in the rectum, and the examination was negative. Her hematocrit was 52, a value felt to be due to dehydration, and her white blood count was 14,000 with a slight shift to the left. Her temperature was 102.4°F. A chest X-ray taken on admission was normal. Films of the abdomen taken 12 hours after admission showed no free intraperitoneal air, but there were numerous loops interpreted as dilated small bowel with thickened walls and intramural air.

In the absence of specific physical findings or dramatic symptoms, the patient was treated supportively with intravenous fluids and antibiotics. Blood chemistries were obtained but were not diagnostic. Her serum amylase was slightly below normal. Her condition remained stable for another 24 hours, then suddenly began to deteriorate. She showed signs of shock. Her white blood count increased to 24,000 with a marked shift to the left, and her temperature rose to 104°F. Her abdomen had become distended. Before additional studies could be performed or surgery decided upon, she had a cardiac arrest and died.

Autopsy revealed massive small intestinal infarction from the proximal jejunum to the ileocecal valve. The cecum and ascending colon were discolored; the remaining colon appeared normal. There was moderate atherosclerosis in the proximal superior mesenteric artery, with severe atherosclerosis and marked narrowing of the proximal inferior mesenteric artery. No thrombi were seen in the arteries, and the abdominal aorta showed no evidence of atherosclerosis. Examination of the portal vein and superior mesenteric vein showed a soft thrombus without organization in the latter. The thrombus had formed before death, as indicated by the presence of lines of Zahn, but was felt to be of quite recent origin and secondary to the bowel infarction.

Suit was filed against all of the attending physicians, alleging failure to diagnose an abdominal emergency and institute prompt therapy.

Discussion and comment. That arterial occlusion of the abdominal viscera can be relatively asymptomatic is recognized but not well appreciated.[1, 2] Undoubtedly this is because the most common cause of intestinal infarction that surgeons see is acute embolization of the superior mesenteric artery—rarely a silent occurrence. Catastrophic abdominal pain in a patient with embolus-prone cardiac disease, when associated with vomiting and bloody diarrhea,[2] is strong evidence of this type of acute vascular surgical emergency.

Yet visceral arterial occlusion can be chronic, and obstruction of a single artery or combination of the three main vessels supplying the viscera can be clinically insidious and indolent.[1-4] When even one of the main intestinal arteries is narrowed, serious intestinal ischemia can gradually develop, accompanied by colicky postprandial abdominal pain, fear of eating, weight loss, and change in bowel habit.

As the occlusive process approaches an emergency situation, fluid loss into the splanchnic bed creates hemoconcentration and hypovolemia. Ultimately infarction occurs. Peritonitis, cardiovascular collapse, and septic shock rapidly ensue, with at least an 80 per cent chance (higher in my experience) of mortality following surgical resection of the necrotic bowel.[2, 3] Perhaps the mortality would be even greater if perforation occurred more often than it does.

Massive resections of small intestine leaving only 18 inches (45.7 cm), and another leaving only 8.3 inches (21 cm), have been reported with successful maintenance of life, but these seem to be extremely rare and unusually fortunate cases.[5, 6] Use of a short reversed segment of jejunum, if feasible, appears to be of more theoretical than actual benefit.[7] I've had no personal experience with the reverse loop.

Intestinal ischemia occurs from the mucosa, which is most vulnerable, outward; actual perforation isn't seen until very late. The chief cause of intestinal ischemia is atherosclerosis, and involvement of the mesenteric vessels is usually spotty and multiple. Because the inferior mesenteric artery is frequently sacrificed during other operations (retroperitoneal lymph node dissections, tumor resections, aortic procedures, etc.) with fewer than 1 per cent of patients exhibiting colon ischemia, its occlusion by vascular disease was thought to be unimportant. As Bergan and his colleagues[1-3] have noted, however, occasionally the inferior mesenteric artery through the arch of Riolan becomes the main source of arterial blood supply to the gut.[4, 8] When, as in this patient, vascular compromise to the small intestine is due to narrowing of both superior and inferior mesenteric arteries, intestinal necrosis should be expected to follow.

This patient's inferior mesenteric artery was severely narrowed, resulting in further diminution of blood supply to the gut through the arch of Riolan. Since some arterial blood was coursing through the superior mesenteric artery, small bowel ischemia was chronic, but additional diminution of flow through the arch of Riolan caused by stenosis of the inferior mesenteric artery was probably enough to cause the catastrophic bowel necrosis. A combination of visceral and mesenteric arterial lesions was at work here. Although no easily definable organic vascular lesion was found at autopsy, severe atherosclerotic narrowing of the main intestinal blood vessels was present and resulted in nonthrombotic intestinal infarction.[3]

With reduced intestinal blood flow, compensatory angiospasm probably occurred, increasing the propensity for intestinal infarction despite the lack of known cardiac disease or low cardiac output in this patient. Unfortunately, the diagnosis of intestinal infarction due to nonthrombotic causes, as in this case, is most difficult to make early, in direct contrast to intestinal infarction caused by acute embolic occlusion.

At autopsy, most of the proximal jejunum, remaining small intestine, and right colon were necrotic. These findings are typical of the chronic, clinically silent processes of mesenteric thrombosis and/or nonthrombotic intestinal infarction rather than of acute embolization.[1, 3] In acute embolization some of the proximal jejunum is frequently spared, as is the right colon. The chronic, clinically silent process can well account for the clinical dilemma confronting the physicians in this case.

The lack of clinical findings and the patient's age and benign appearance were misleading and masked the insidious progression of the disease as well as its exact nature. However, X-rays showing dilated intestinal loops and intramural air were highly suggestive of small bowel necrosis, and increasing white blood counts and temperature were corroborative. Even though the patient's clinical picture apparently didn't indicate surgical intervention, massive small intestinal necrosis had already occurred and the right colon was also compromised. Successful outcome following surgical resection and revascularization would appear doubtful.[1]

References

1. Bergan JJ, Dean RH, Conn J Jr, et al: Revascularization in treatment of mesenteric infarction. *Ann Surg* 182:430, 1975
2. Bergan JJ, Yao JST: Acute mesenteric artery thrombosis. In *Davis-Christopher Textbook of Surgery* (Sabiston DC, ed), 11th ed, p 1992. Philadelphia: Saunders, 1977
3. Bergan JJ: Recognition and treatment of intestinal ischemia. *Surg Clin North Am* 47:109, 1967
4. Ruzicka FF Jr, Rossi P: Normal vascular anatomy of the abdominal viscera. *Radiol Clin North Am* 8:1, 1970
5. Berman LG: Metabolic studies of an unusual case of survival following resection of all but 18 inches of small intestine. *Ann Surg* 132:64, 1950
6. Bothe FA, Magee WS, Driscoll RH: A massive resection of the small intestine from 15 cm. distal to the ligament of Treitz to within 6 cm. of the ileocecal valve. *Ann Surg* 140:755, 1954
7. Gibson LD, Carter R, Hinshaw DB: Segmental reversal of small intestine after massive bowel resection. *JAMA* 182:952, 1962
8. Owen K, Rob CG: Ligation of the coeliac and superior mesenteric arteries. *Arch Surg* 84:95, 1956

42

Melanoma, regressed and regressing

A 34-year-old woman consulted her family physician because of a lump in her left armpit of two months' duration. She also had noticed that a mole on the skin of her upper back, just to the left of the midline, had become raised and changed color from tan to greenish black. On initial examination the left axilla contained a freely movable, solitary, firm, nontender tumor about 2.5 cm in size. The mole on the back was slightly raised and approximately 1.5 cm across, with fuzzy or hazy margins. It was said to have been darker before the initial visit.

The mole was totally excised. The pathology report was "benign junctional nevus with active junctional change." In view of this report, no attention was paid to the left axillary tumor, which was the chief reason for the patient's visit to the doctor. The tumor grew and finally was removed two months after her first visit. The pathology report was "undifferentiated carcinoma, metastatic." There was no pigment present.

Because there was no other likely site of a primary cancer, the slide of the previously removed mole was reviewed, this time by another pathologist. In his opinion, the mole was an "incipient, invasive, superficial spreading melanoma extending to a depth of 0.3 mm or to a Clark's Level II."[1] Classification as benign or malignant on the basis of microscopic appearance was considered exceedingly difficult. But that the left axillary tumor was a metastasis from the now "malignant mole" was deemed beyond doubt.

The absence of pigment in the metastatic axillary node did not preclude a melanoma as the primary source of disease. Not infrequently a melanoma metastasis will not be pigmented, as its rapid growth will have outstripped the formation of pigment. An axillary dissection was performed; no other nodes were involved. Although the patient was alive and well a year later, suit was filed against the family physician, alleging failure to diagnose and also delay in diagnosing cancer.

Discussion and comment. This case clearly illustrates the difficulty in histologic interpretation of a melanoma or an active junctional nevus.[2, 3] A jury of six expert pathologists reviewing the microscopic slide of this patient's melanoma would probably be evenly divided between the verdicts of benign and malignant. The physician was vulnerable, however, because the enlarged lymph node, the complaint that brought the patient to consult him in the first place, was ignored too long. Furthermore, the lymph node did not become enlarged suddenly. The change in character of the mole on the left upper back, which is in the lymphatic drainage area of the left axilla, should have alerted the physician to the overall clinical picture. Had he removed the node mass at the same time as the mole, the nature of this patient's tumor would have been no mystery. Even though the overall prognosis might not have been changed, exposure to malpractice liability would have been less.

The differing histologic interpretations of the mole deserve further comment. Metastatic melanoma without a primary tumor is occasionally found in the lymphatic drainage area of a previously excised "benign" mole.[4] Such a mole has been described as a "regressed or regressing melanoma."[5-8] To qualify as a regressed melanoma, in the view of Smith and Stehlin,[7] the skin in question, usually a fine white scar or a faintly blue, translucent area, must (1) correspond to the location of a once-pigmented lesion that has changed its appearance over a period of time, (2) occur in a lymphatic bed drained by lymph nodes containing the metastases, and (3) show no evidence of primary malignant melanoma.

Regressing melanomas—i.e., melanomas in partial regression—also occur, perhaps in 10 to 15 per cent of malignant melanomas.[8] Histologically, regressive changes are frequently found at the dermal-epidermal junction around areas of infiltration. Residual primary melanoma, intraepithelial and dermal, still is present, in contrast to a regressed melanoma.

The equivocal histologic appearance of the primary melanoma in this case can now be explained. Metastases to the left axillary nodes had occurred during an earlier, aggressive phase of this melanoma. At the time the mole was excised it was in partial regression, with a histologic appearance that was "benign" or "incipient, invasive"—a stage where lymph node metastasis would not be expected.[9] Such a pathology report clouded the clinical picture. There was no breach in an acceptable standard of care. Unfortunately, these circumstances do not mitigate malpractice exposure in this case.

References

1. Clark WH, From L, Bernardino EA, et al: The histogenesis and biologic behavior of primary human malignant melanomas of the skin. *Cancer Res* 29:705, 1969
2. Little JH: Histology and prognosis in cutaneous malignant melanoma. In *Melanoma and Skin Cancer, Proceedings of the International Cancer Conference (Sydney)*, pp 107-120. Sydney: Blight, Government Printer, 1972
3. Price NM, Rywlin AM, Ackerman AB: Histologic criteria for the diagnosis of superficial spreading malignant melanoma: Formulated on the basis of proven metastatic lesions. *Cancer* 38:2434, 1976
4. Bowden L: Spontaneous regression of malignant melanoma. In *13th Congressus Internationalis Dermatologiae (München)*, pp 918-925. Berlin: Springer, 1968
5. Das Gupta T, Bowden L, Berg JW: Malignant melanoma of unknown primary site. *Surg Gynecol Obstet* 117:341, 1963
6. Reed R: *New Concepts of Surgical Pathology of the Skin.* New York: Wiley, 1976
7. Smith LJ, Stehlin JS: Spontaneous regression of primary malignant melanomas with regional metastases. *Cancer* 18:1399, 1965
8. Woodruff JM: Pathology of malignant melanoma. II. *Memorial Sloan-Kettering Cancer Center Clin Bull* 6:(2)52, 1976
9. McGovern VG: Melanoma: Growth patterns, multiplicity and regression. In *Melanoma and Skin Cancer, Proceedings of the International Cancer Conference (Sydney)*, pp 95-106. Sydney: Blight, Government Printer, 1972

43

Fat embolism syndrome (post-traumatic pulmonary insufficiency)

When his small airplane crashed, a 30-year-old man experienced numerous injuries over his entire body but had no bruise or contusion marks on the face or head. Physical examination revealed multiple, bilateral rib fractures with an anterior chest injury of the crush, deceleration type, more marked on the left. Both bones of the left forearm were fractured, as well as both femurs. His breathing was labored, but his airway appeared patent and adequate. Although in semishock, he could be roused and did respond to questioning. There was no easily discernible swelling about the fracture sites that would denote occult hemorrhage. His respiratory motion showed an isolated "flail" or floating segment composed of the fractured ribs on the left side.

X-ray examinations of the patient's chest revealed an elevated, presumably paralyzed left diaphragm, widening of the upper mediastinum with loss of sharpness of the contour of the aortic knob, and suspected left hemothorax without evidence of pneumothorax. His cardiac silhouette was enlarged, but no cardiac tamponade was evident. He had a mild left hemiplegia, and a paralyzed left vocal cord was noted during passage of an endotracheal tube to start positive pressure breathing.

Because of the violent, deceleration type of accident, the nature of the multiple rib fractures with an associated floating segment, and the chest X-rays, which suggested an aortic rupture, aortography was immediately carried out. It revealed an aortic tear posteriorly at the point where the aorta passes from its mediastinal location to a retropleural one. This is the location of the ligamentum arteriosum and is the point of fixation of the aorta. The patient did not exhibit unequal pulses and blood pressures in the extremities or complain of excruciating pain—signs and symptoms that would have suggested a beginning dissecting aneurysm.

In proper sequence, a patent airway was assured and hemorrhage and shock were at least temporarily controlled with Ringer's lactate solution, 1.25 per cent albumin in a balanced salt solution, and dextran 40 (Rheomacrodex). The fractures were splinted. A central venous pressure line was placed in position through the right subclavian vein and an indwelling catheter placed in the urinary bladder. Pulse rate and arterial blood pressure were carefully monitored.

Surgical intervention was prompt: The thorax was entered, the aortic rupture repaired, and the flail segment of chest wall stabilized as well as could be. A tracheostomy was performed. The patient's general condition was good enough to permit an abdominal exploration also, since preoperative peritoneal taps were somewhat ambiguous. Celiotomy was negative. The fractures were placed in casts, but both femurs were immobilized in traction. He was started on antibiotics as a prophylactic measure.

The patient's postoperative course was amazingly stable. He was comfortably out of shock and did nicely under close monitoring during the first 48 hours. The tracheostomy facilitated positive pressure ventilation. The central venous pressure line was carefully watched, and his venous as well as arterial pressure remained stable. A nasogastric suction tube was employed as well as thoracotomy drainage, and a Foley urinary catheter was placed on direct bottle drainage. Adequate fluid replacement, now with low molecular weight dextran, and blood replacement, depending on blood volume and urinary output, were maintained. ECG monitoring, repeated portable chest X-rays, and antibiotics were continued.

Problems started on the third postoperative day and were typical of the syndrome of fat embolism and/or post-traumatic pulmonary insufficiency. Since the patient had previously been progressing satisfactorily, a fat embolism syndrome (FES) seemed more likely.

Tachycardia, tachypnea, and fever all increased, and a petechial rash developed, chiefly over the upper trunk and axillae and on the conjunctiva. Arterial blood gases showed a drop in pO_2, indicative of arterial hypoxemia, and the chest X-rays showed a fluffy, diffuse infiltrate in the lungs. The patient's hematocrit fell, as did platelets. Some fat globules were seen in the retinal vessels.

The patient became confused, then semicomatose—in the absence of an obvious head injury, a significant and ominous finding in FES. Serum lipase increased, and neutral fat was noted in the urine. Fat globules were easily demonstrated in a rapid-frozen section clot (cryostat).[1]

Vigorous ventilatory support using a volume respirator was

continued, and positive end-expiratory pressure was added to this in hopes of increasing functional residual capacity and decreasing pulmonary shunting. Intravenous corticosteroids were started. Serum albumin was administered to the patient to keep the level above 3.5 gm/100 ml. Ethyl alcohol (5 per cent) intravenously, which has been shown to inhibit lipase activity, was not utilized, nor was heparin, although heparin does have "lipemic" clearing and anticlotting capabilities.[2-6]

Despite these heroic measures, the patient's condition went rapidly downhill. His coma deepened, and although his cardiopulmonary system was kept functional, his "brain died" and he became cyanotic over the next 36 hours. Cardiac arrest followed shortly. An autopsy was not performed.

Suit was filed against all physicians in attendance, alleging failure to take measures to prevent, alleviate, and/or attenuate a fat embolism syndrome.

Discussion and comment. Post-traumatic pulmonary insufficiency,[2-5, 7, 8] fat embolism syndrome, adult respiratory distress phenomenon, and "shocked lung" all describe the hypoxemia that often follows a serious injury, even though the site of injury may be far removed from the lungs. Hypoxemia continues to be a significant cause of death following accidents. Although the almost overwhelming nature of this patient's multiple injuries was enough to cast doubt on his survival, FES was a precipitating factor in his death.

FES isn't always associated with trauma or accidents. Intramedullary pinning may be a cause in itself. It may occur in association with diabetes, burns, severe infections, inhalation anesthesia, metabolic disorders, soft tissue injury, neoplasms, osteomyelitis, blood transfusions, cardiopulmonary bypass, decompression to altitude, renal infarction, renal homotransplantation, steroid-induced fatty liver, and sickle cell disease.[7]

According to the mechanical theory of FES, fat emboli arise from the marrow at the site of fracture and are carried to the pulmonary capillary bed. There they cause temporary occlusion of the small vessels, which in turn causes hemorrhage and ischemic changes in the lung tissue.[1-3, 9, 10]

From a physiochemical standpoint, Lehmann and Moore[8] have attributed the pulmonary, cutaneous, and cerebral pathology to the toxic effects of free fatty acids.[2, 3, 11] The source of these free fatty acids may be hydrolysis of neutral fat droplets by tissue lipase and/or the mobilization of fatty acid stores by catecholamines, glucagon, or steroids.[2, 3] The free fatty acids exert a toxic effect on lung tissue, disrupting the capillary alveolar membrane and altering surfactant activity, which leads to frothy edema, hemorrhage, and further loss of functional residual capacity.[2, 3, 5, 7, 8, 11]

In the normal state free fatty acids are transported through the intravascular space, bound principally to albumin. Following injury free fatty acid levels are significantly elevated, to an extent proportionate to the magnitude of the injury. The source of excess fatty acids, as noted, seems to be lipolysis of adipose tissue, producing excessive lipid mobilization.[2-4, 7, 12, 13]

According to Moylan,[2-4, 13] patients who develop FES have a lower serum albumin than those who don't. Albumin given intravenously soon after trauma reduces the level of unbound free fatty acids and decreases the incidence of FES in multiple injuries.

This patient exhibited most of the diagnostic features of FES, and they characteristically occurred on the third postaccident day. Dyspnea, mental confusion, petechiae, tachypnea progressing to severe dyspnea, and cyanosis were all present. Onset on the third day following the accident helped differentiate FES in this patient from other causes of respiratory distress (e.g., pulmonary contusion). "Shocked lung" supposedly occurs later in the postinjury period (fifth day), but the similarity between this state and FES is clear.

Chest X-rays reveal "fluffy densities" in the lungs. Urinary (or sputum) fat globules are not reliable but are helpful diagnostic signs. Many patients have urinary fat globules following major trauma whether they have respiratory distress or not. Moylan and Evenson[3] feel that the absence of fat globules in the urine of patients with respiratory distress makes the diagnosis of fat emboli unlikely and points more toward "shocked lung." They noted that the latter causes respiratory distress about five days after injury. By that time fat is absent from the urine. Other doubtful or merely suggestive signs of FES are thrombocytopenia, hypofibrinogenemia, and prolonged partial thromboplastin time, but these are more likely due to hypovolemic shock than to FES.[2-5, 7] Serum lipase and tributyrinase levels have not been corroborative.

The chief tool in diagnosis of FES is arterial blood gases. A pO_2 less than 60 mm Hg on room air indicates significant oxygen desaturation and the need for respiratory support. Hyperventilation may make the pCO_2 low initially and the patient slightly alkalotic. As the lung condition deteriorates with continued hypoxia, hypercapnia and acidosis develop.

Treatment of this patient followed well-laid-down principles. All fractures were stabilized promptly and hypovolemia controlled quickly despite imminent aortic rupture. These are obvious essential initial considerations.

Low molecular weight dextran, which was given during the early post-trauma period, was recommended by Evarts[7] in the treatment of FES. According to Evarts, low molecular weight dextran will induce expansion of the plasma volume, cause formation of a dextran-fibrinogen complex, alter the surface charge of erythrocytes, and exert a siliconizing effect on injured blood vessel walls. Intravenous administration of 500 ml every 12 hours reduces the intravascular aggregation of erythrocytes, increases blood fluidity, improves capillary flow, and increases tissue perfusion. Its use is recommended until the patient is symptom-free, but contraindications exist: pulmonary edema, congestive heart failure, renal failure, severe dehydration, thrombocytopenia, hypofibrinogenemia, and a localized septic process.[7] Moylan[2, 3] has questioned the value of low molecular weight dextran and would seem to prefer albumin for its fatty acid-binding properties as well as its capability as a volume expander.

In this patient, hidden blood loss was taken into account and close monitoring and continued observation employed (central venous pressure, fluid intake and output, hematocrit, chest X-rays, close inspection of fracture sites, etc.). Albumin was used for its fatty acid-binding property (maintaining a level above 3.5 gm/100 ml), and corticosteroids in high doses were given. Their anti-inflammatory property is believed to be the reason why corticosteroids reverse the toxic effects of excess free fatty acids.[2, 14]

Heparin was not used in this patient because of the danger of initiating or enhancing further hemorrhage. Its use in patients with multiple skeletal and soft tissue injuries, as well as vascular damage, is a difficult decision to make.[6] Heparin has long been known to exert a chylolytic or clearing action by facilitating the passage of chylomicrons into the tissues.[6, 7] It also increases serum lipase action and thus hastens intravascular hydrolysis of neutral fat. Its anticoagulant action may promote microcirculatory flow. Evarts[7] recommended small intravenous injections of 1,000 to 5,000 USP units of sodium heparin every six to eight hours—a dose he considered would not increase the risk of hemorrhage. According to Evarts, a patient with multiple injuries may be given this dosage shortly after hospital admission;[7] one should not wait for a petechial rash to develop. Trunkey et al[6] recommended low doses of heparin (2,500 to 5,000 units) every six hours intravenously after bleeding has ceased. However, they were concerned more with emboli of hematogenous origin, not fat emboli. In this patient, with an aortic tear and other injuries, heparin initially would appear to have been contraindicated.

Ventilation and respiratory support with a volume respirator are often essential to maintain the arterial pO_2 at 70 mm Hg or better. Nasal oxygen all too frequently will not attain this desired level. High tidal volumes (in the range of 15 ml/kg) are effective in stabilizing and reversing pulmonary post-traumatic respiratory distress. Positive end-expiratory pressure is beneficial in increasing the functional residual capacity and decreasing pulmonary shunting in these patients.[2-4, 14]

It isn't clear whether the charges of malpractice in this case have real merit. Multisystem injuries still carry a high mortality. Sevitt[11] reported 80 per cent mortality in accidents of this type. Mortality is also high in patients with FES, more so in comatose patients than in those without cerebral symptoms and signs.[7] How much residual subclinical brain damage this patient might have sustained is unknown, but it could have contributed to his death along with the cerebral involvement due to FES.

The failure to make use of prophylactic corticosteroids, albumin, or even heparin can hardly be grounds for suit in such a severely injured patient. The FES was promptly recognized and treated when it occurred. Whether use of these agents before the third day after the accident would have prevented, alleviated, and/or attenuated the effects and accumulation of fat emboli and the ensuing syndrome is highly debatable and does not appear to be a reasonable allegation.

References

1. Lahiri B, ZuWallack R: The early diagnosis and treatment of fat embolism syndrome: A preliminary report. *J Trauma* 17:956, 1977
2. Moylan JA, Evenson MA: Diagnosis and treatment of fat embolism. *Ann Rev Med* 28:85, 1977
3. Moylan JA: Fat embolism syndrome. In *Davis-Christopher Textbook of Surgery* (Sabiston DC, ed), 11th ed, pp 1860-1863. Philadelphia: Saunders, 1977
4. Moylan JA, Birnbaum M, Katz A, et al: Fat emboli syndrome. *J Trauma* 16:341, 1976
5. Pollak R, Myers RAM: Early diagnosis of the fat embolism syndrome. *J Trauma* 18:121, 1978
6. Trunkey DD, Chapman MW, Lim RC Jr, et al: Management of pelvic fractures in blunt trauma injury. *J Trauma* 14:912, 1974
7. Evarts CM: The fat embolism syndrome: A review. *Surg Clin North Am* 50:493, 1970
8. Lehmann EP, Moore RM: Fat embolism including experimental production without trauma. *Arch Surg* 14:621, 1927
9. Arnim J, Grant RE: Observations on gross pulmonary fat embolism in man and in the rabbit. *Can J Surg* 9:286, 1966
10. Gauss H: The pathology of fat embolism. *Arch Surg* 9:593, 1924
11. Sevitt S: *Fat Embolism,* p 143. London: Butterworths, 1962
12. Knowles GD, Putnam CE, Smith W, et al: Fat embolism associated with an atrial septal defect. *J Trauma* 16:71, 1976
13. Editorial: Preventing fat embolism. *Br Med J* 1:1232, 1978
14. Ashbaugh DG, Petty TL: The use of corticosteroids in the treatment of respiratory failure associated with massive fat embolism. *Surg Gynecol Obstet* 123:493, 1966

Section IV

A legal primer

This section is not an exhaustive text on medical malpractice law. It isn't necessary or practical for most physicians to know everything there is to know about malpractice. Leave that to your insurance carrier and a capable attorney.

The chances that you'll ever be sued or subpoenaed to testify in a malpractice case are probably slight. But there are basic things you need to know to protect yourself if the need should arise. Look on the following chapters, therefore, as a practical primer.

44

You and the jury

"We finally agreed to give her something, but I'm still sorry it wasn't twice as much. A doctor like that deserves a real lesson. Before he was on the stand two minutes I could tell he was trying to cover up heaven knows what. And imagine a doctor keeping a patient's record on a tiny little card; why, it's ridiculous!"

The speaker was a 52-year-old homemaker, juror No. 7 in a malpractice suit lost by a surgeon. Her remarks were addressed to an insurance company investigator, a man who has interviewed hundreds of jurors after trials involving doctors his company insures. He has found that malpractice jurors judge a doctor's innocence or guilt from many aspects, some of which have nothing to do with formal points of the law. He's pinpointed five important areas:

1. *The defendant's professional knowledge.* Faced with two doctors of equal skill who are defendants in similar malpractice suits, the jury is apt to acquit the one who seems more professionally knowledgeable. After a large suit in which an obstetrician-gynecologist was completely exonerated, no fewer than eight members of the jury stressed that "he really keeps up with advances in medicine" and "he knows his stuff inside out." "I just don't believe," said the jury foreman, "that a man as well informed as he is would have done that if it hadn't been the best thing to do."

By contrast, in another malpractice suit tried the same year, a general practitioner lost a verdict partly because he struck the jury as having a poor medical education and because his office records, charts, and files on the patient were scanty and illegible. One juror noted, "His lawyer would have talked about his education if it was worth talking about. I can recognize ignorance when I see it . . . and those records!"

2. *The defendant's regard for the truth.* If jury members think the doctor and his witnesses are more concerned with getting at the

truth than they are with avoiding responsibility, they may decide to acquit or at least hold down the amount of any award.

One case stands out as a stunning example of what *not* to do. The defendant, a chief of service, had given an injection that resulted in the plaintiff's paralysis. In court he denied he was to blame. "I took a completely normal risk," he said. He and a group of expert witnesses insisted the patient's condition was hopeless anyway. Doctor after doctor testified that "this man has only one to two years to live." Therefore, they pointedly added, his remaining expenses were bound to be modest. To the jury it was all too obvious that the doctors' motive was to rule out any possibility of a big award if the case should be lost.

The jurors decided that the doctors were lying. "That was rehearsed testimony if I ever heard any," one juror commented afterward. He and his fellow jurors decided the plaintiff would probably live 10 years more and awarded him a large judgment. But only two years and one month after the trial the plaintiff died.

In a similar suit, brought jointly against a doctor and a hospital over a death following an injection, the physician answered all questions with an evident desire to establish the truth. This time it was the hospital nurses who made a poor impression on the jury. They took the stand chiefly, according to one juror, "to make pious disclaimers." The result was exoneration for the physician but a verdict against the hospital.

3. *The defendant's concern for the welfare of his patient.* "Even though she was suing him," said a juror in a malpractice suit, "we felt the doctor was still treating that woman right in court." "He's the kind of man who deals with patients, not just symptoms," said another. The suit resulted in a verdict for the defendant.

4. *The doctor's willingness to learn from a mistake.* If the jurors feel a doctor has learned a lesson from his error, they may vote for his acquittal. If they think he's apt to shrug the whole thing off and make the same mistake again, they're more likely to find him guilty.

Take two almost parallel suits, both alleging damage to a baby during delivery. In one case, which was decided for the doctor, the jury was almost unanimous in thinking the doctor had learned from the case. As one juror said: "He was frank enough to say he probably should have waited another hour to 'knock' the mother out, in spite of her pains. I liked him for that, and I'm sure he'll know better next time." In the other case, the jury brought in a verdict against the doctor defendant. "He just sat there like a mule, denying everything," said the foreman. "You got the feeling he'd do the same thing again tomorrow. Aside from the parents' just claim, he needed a lesson." The self-righteous urge to "teach that doctor a lesson" is very evident on the part of some of today's juries.

5. *The defendant's demeanor on the stand.* Jurors are likely to be favorably impressed by a physician who avoids sarcasm, condescension, or undue levity. One defendant was asked to explain how a woman became pregnant after he had performed a vasectomy on her husband, the plaintiff. The doctor said, "She must have been seeing too much of the iceman." He got a laugh but he also alienated the jury, especially the four women on it. The verdict wound up against him.

That doesn't mean that all jurors are impressed by, or even understand, medical testimony. In today's malpractice trials the medical issues are often complex and sophisticated and may demand more than average lay insight. Nonetheless, it's wisest to follow one experienced attorney's advice: "Some jurors *are* stupid. But you'd better not act as if you think so. Don't ever talk down to them. Address those 12 men and women as your peers, and you just about double the effectiveness of your testimony."

What's true for physician defendants also applies to the plaintiff's side. And plaintiffs' lawyers have a built-in advantage if they can find a piece of dramatic visual evidence to sway jurors' emotions. Take the case of a doctor charged with the death of a child from hemorrhage following a tonsillectomy. The child's parents claimed that the doctor had ignored the results of preoperative blood coagulation and clotting tests suggesting that the patient was likely to bleed excessively. Their lawyer was not content with presenting oral testimony to back up that charge. He kept the jury's attention focused on "Exhibit A," a pair of bloodstained child's pajamas. The result was an award for the plaintiff.

There's little a defendant can do about the impression the plaintiff makes on the jury. But he can do a great deal about the jury's impression of him. If he conducts himself as a thoughtful, conscientious, forthright medical scientist, most jurors will give his case a fair, and even sympathetic, hearing.

45

On the witness stand

Even though you may be fortunate enough to avoid being the defendant in a malpractice case, you're increasingly likely to be called as a witness. When your turn comes, will your pretrial preparations be adequate? Will your testimony have the best possible effect? Will you be able to survive vigorous cross-examination?

Although you're only a witness, *you are on trial*. What you say not only bears heavily on the outcome of the case but also reflects on your personal honesty, reputation, and professional ability.

To be an effective witness, you must, above all, be prepared. Without adequate preparation, you may have your forensic hide torn by an able trial lawyer. Thorough preparation can make your testimony virtually invincible. Whenever you're in doubt about legal duties as a medical witness, consult your own attorney. He can tell you what pretrial steps to take and what you should know about the laws governing appearance in court. Here are basic guidelines:

In any legal matter, always double-check requests for information. When a lawyer asks for information on a patient, don't give it until you have obtained written permission from your patient and from the person or company the lawyer claims to represent. Shortly after a suit was filed against a Wisconsin physician, he received a call from an attorney who claimed to represent his insurance carrier. The lawyer asked the doctor to send him all records pertaining to the case. The doctor obliged. He subsequently discovered, to his horror, that the attorney was actually the plaintiff's counsel.

Whomever an attorney represents, remember that he cannot compel you to tell him anything unless you are under subpoena, and then only after you have been sworn in as a witness. Lawyers, of course, prefer you to be sympathetic and cooperative. As a matter of professional courtesy most of them will ask you to produce records or testify voluntarily.

If you exercise your right to refuse, an attorney may then ask the court to issue a subpoena. When properly served, this document makes it mandatory that you surrender your records to the clerk of the court from which it was issued, appear in court as a witness, or both. Failure to comply with a subpoena constitutes contempt of court. In most jurisdictions, you are legally summoned if the process server merely sees you and drops the summons on the ground in front of you. Generally he must see *you;* he can't leave a subpoena with your spouse or secretary.

Service of the subpoena, however, doesn't put you at the mercy of the lawyer or the court. In many states you cannot be compelled to appear as a witness if you live beyond a given number of miles from the court. A subpoena is invalid in most states unless statutory witness and transportation fees are paid, if requested, at the time of service. The amounts are usually nominal, a few dollars, and are not to be confused with professional witness fees agreed upon with the lawyer. Subpoenas served across state lines are usually invalid.

Although you must answer any subpoena, you can obtain a postponement if you submit a valid reason, such as personal illness, surgery that cannot be delayed, or a death in the family. Without the judge's permission to be absent you will face contempt-of-court proceedings. You may, with the consent of the plaintiff and defendant, arrange to testify entirely in a pretrial deposition.

You may be called either as a medical fact witness, to give testimony on what you *saw and did,* or as a medical expert or opinion witness, to discuss what, in your well-informed opinion, *could or should have been done.*

As a rule, the expert witness comes under heavier interrogatory pressure than the physician who is reporting facts. Consequently, his preparation and testimony are usually more exacting. These points are important:

- To testify as an expert, you do not have to be a specialist. Your license to practice qualifies you to testify on any medical matter. This rule is under some question in today's medicolegal environment, but it still applies.
- You cannot be forced to indulge in guesswork. If you honestly haven't formed an opinion or are not sure of your ground, say so. Your honesty will probably win you points with the jury.
- You will probably be asked to describe in detail your experience and qualifications. Prepare for this before going to court.
- If you are testifying as an expert, you are free to give opinions, prognoses, and evaluations. But if you are a fact witness, you must limit your testimony to objective facts. Be certain you know whether

you are appearing as a fact witness or an expert witness. Have a firm commitment on the subjects your testimony will cover. In court, if you should get a question you haven't prepared for, admit it. You may explain your reasons to the court if you wish. Don't hedge; be completely candid.

As an expert witness, you are generally entitled to a fee—not for your testimony, but for your time. Some states permit expert witnesses to be compensated for their testimony, but even if you're preparing to testify in a state that does, you're better off not charging for your services as an expert. Your image as a "hired witness" will work against you. It is, however, entirely proper—and expected—for you to be paid for your time spent in preparing testimony, advising the attorney, and sitting in court. You should arrange for payment by drawing up a contract with the attorney, specifying what you'll be paid for and the hourly rate you'll charge. Under no circumstances should you make your fee contingent on the amount of the award.

As a fact witness, you are entitled to the statutory witness fee, paid by the court—usually a few dollars, as mentioned earlier. But if you must spend considerable time reviewing your records and sitting in court, you may be entitled to extra compensation. Often attorneys offer it; it's also appropriate for you to request it.

Just as a court may issue a subpoena for your person, it may seize and examine your records. You are likely to suffer considerable embarrassment if those records are not properly prepared. The physician with incomplete, poorly kept, or out-of-date records is inviting brutal cross-examination. Opposing counsel knows he can seriously damage his adversary's case by discrediting your testimony. If the condition of your records forces you to rely on memory, you're apt to find yourself making one inconsistent statement after another. Moreover, jurors tend to put themselves in the patient's shoes. They feel that a physician should accurately record every fact concerning diagnosis and treatment. They will even relate missing or sloppy records to loss of life.

For court purposes, well-kept records should include:

1. All pertinent dates
2. The circumstances that brought the patient to you for treatment
3. The patient's comments on his case, i.e., his physical complaints, and a thorough history
4. Findings of the physical examination
5. Presumptive diagnosis and discharge diagnosis
6. Auxiliary diagnostic aids used (X-rays, laboratory tests, consultations, etc.) and their results

7. Type of treatment
8. Details of each step of treatment
9. Appropriate consent forms
10. Financial statements for services rendered.

If the diagnosis is uncertain, it should be labeled "presumptive" or "provisional." If your knowledge of the circumstances surrounding the patient's illness or injury is based solely on what he told you, be sure it's recorded as hearsay, and not as fact.

How's your handwriting? Trial lawyers frequently complain of medical witnesses who can't read their own records. In the eyes of the jury, slovenly writing is an indication of how you practice medicine.

What about mistakes in your records? Assume you check records you haven't seen in years and find an error. Your first inclination is to blot it out or erase it. Don't. Instead, draw a thin line—in ink—through the mistake, write the correct information directly above it, and date and initial the correction. When on the witness stand, inform the court of the mistake before you discuss the records. This is the only way to avoid the embarrassing inference that your records were tailored specifically for the trial.

Before you take the witness stand you should have a pretrial consultation to review the bill of particulars with the attorney who wants you to testify. Contrary to the opinion still held by some, a discussion of the case before the trial is ethically correct as well as invaluable to courtroom strategy. Moreover, if the attorney doesn't take the initiative and arrange a meeting reasonably ahead of the trial, you take it. You must make sure that your role as a witness is clearly spelled out. The witness stand is no place for surprises.

Once you and the attorney have agreed on the scope of your testimony, study all the pertinent material available. If possible, examine the patient or review the autopsy report. Bear in mind that the court wants *your* opinion. After studying your sources thoroughly, form your own conclusions.

What you have said in pretrial depositions or as an expert witness in other trials is also important. Remember those remarks before you take the stand. The cross-examiner will be searching for discrepancies to discredit your testimony by slighting your reputation as an expert.

The way a medical witness appears on the stand can carry as much weight with a jury as his or her actual testimony. Jurors may let their opinions be swayed by a doctor's appearance. They expect him or her to be neat and conservatively dressed, to sit up straight, and to act calm.

While you wait to be called to the stand, sit quietly. The less attention you attract, the better. To keep the wait before being called to testify as brief as possible, ask the lawyer to phone you shortly before you're due to take the stand.

Also, while sitting in the courtroom, don't engage in conversation with anyone. A person you assume is an idle spectator might turn out to be a witness for the other side.

When your name is called, quietly take the stand. Clearly reply "I do" to the oath and give your name, address, and occupation.

Next, you'll probably be asked to state your professional qualifications. They can add considerable authority to your testimony. This is no time for puffery—but also no time for false modesty. List your degrees and tell where and when you obtained them. Mention your specialty, board certification, any additional studies, general experience, all staff and teaching positions, publications, and research projects. If you've written anything especially relevant to the subject you will testify on, mention that too. Anything that gives the impression you know what you're talking about should be included in your qualifications.

When you take the stand, bring your records with you. Courts in most states will not let you read them directly, but you may ask the judge for permission to refer to them. Do not, however, bring textbooks and other reference matter to the stand. Only on rare occasions will a judge permit you to read outside source material. Even more important, bringing source material to the stand or quoting a specific expert makes you vulnerable to minute cross-examination. Study your sources thoroughly before the trial. Then leave them at home.

On the stand, remember that although the attorneys ask the questions, your answers are primarily for the jurors. Direct your testimony to them. Look interested, speak with conviction, and above all, take your time. If you rush, you'll give the impression that you were too well rehearsed. Worse, you may make mistakes.

Remember that the average American juror understands medical language about as well as he understands Chinese. Therefore, avoid technical terms. Say "swelling," not "edema"; "black and blue," not "ecchymosis"; "injury," not "trauma." Make what you say interesting as well as informative. If you're describing a neurologic examination, for example, take the jury through it step by step and explain the significance of each test performed. Use analogies, such as likening the brain to an intricate control room and the nerves to a communications system.

Answer questions briefly and to the point. Volunteering additional information will leave you open to some uncomfortable cross-examination. Equally important, make sure you understand every question. If an attorney mumbles or uses an ambiguous phrase, or if you simply don't understand what he's after, ask him to repeat or rephrase the question until it's crystal clear. If you have insufficient information on a subject, admit it. Guessing may get you in trouble with the opposing lawyer.

Cross-examination is often the most maddening part of a court appearance. Even if you are well prepared and have made a good showing under direct examination, the opposing attorney's tactics may unnerve you. You can't help thinking that his primary aim is to discredit your testimony and raise doubts about your integrity and ability. You're probably correct.

The battle of wits begins when your counsel completes his questioning and says, "Cross-examine." If the opposing counsel's reply is a tart "No questions," your answers under direct examination were probably irrefutable. No lawyer wants damaging testimony repeated. More often, though, the opposing counsel believes he can weaken what you have said, in which case he'll take you on.

He may try to create doubt in the jurors' minds by discrediting you personally. For instance, he may ask: "Doctor, have you discussed this case with anyone?" If you hem and haw, the cross-examiner will be delighted. He'll have the jury suspicious of you already. The correct answer, of course, is "Yes."

Another tricky question: "Doctor, how much are you being paid for your testimony?" Opposing counsel knows you are probably getting a fee. He would like the jury to think that you're being paid to testify. Your answer, however, should be "Nothing." If he pursues the issue, tell him you're not getting a cent for your testimony; you are being reimbursed for the time you spent away from your practice.

If the cross-examiner cannot discredit you personally, he may try to assail your professional qualifications. Assume, for example, that an intricate neurologic matter is introduced during a trial. If you're a pediatrician, you cannot honestly claim to be an expert on neurology. In case you try it, opposing counsel will have a field day with you. Admit that you are out of your depth. The jury will respect your honesty.

In another effort to trip you, the cross-examiner may refer to the opinions of other experts. He may begin by asking you to name some authoritative works on the subject at issue. You mention three or four. When you come to the one he has in mind, he stops you and produces a copy. For the jury's benefit he describes the author and his writings as invaluable assets to medical science. Then you're brought back into the act.

"Would you say that Dr. So-and-So is one of the authorities on the subject?" he asks.

"I would."

"And this book is used throughout the world as a classic text?"

"Yes, I believe so." From now on the jury will expect your testimony to be consistent with all of Dr. So-and-So's opinions.

"Doctor, this is what Dr. So-and-So says, and I quote. . . ." The attorney then reads a passage that seems to contradict your testimony. Then he asks, "Is this a sound medical statement? Please answer Yes or No."

Don't be tricked. In this case neither "Yes" nor "No" is an adequate answer. This is your cue to turn to the judge for permission to give a more complete answer. If he grants permission, as judges usually do in such situations, you have a chance to explain away the apparent conflict. If you can do so satisfactorily, a wise cross-examiner will quickly drop that line of questioning. If the judge does not grant your request, simply reply, "I do not agree with that passage." You'll get a chance later on, in the rebuttal, to reaffirm your earlier testimony.

Never let the cross-examiner lull you into a sense of security. Remember, no matter how polite he is, the opposing attorney's real aim is to lessen the impact of your testimony. That is his job. Pay strict attention to every word he says. If a question is ambiguous, ask him to clarify it. If it's complex, separate it into its parts and give appropriate answers to each.

How to survive cross-examination does not depend solely on the astuteness of your answers. There are other rules of conduct to remember:

- Maintain your poise. Do not fidget, lose your temper, or become argumentative.
- Take your time testifying.
- Do not volunteer information.
- Speak clearly and succinctly.
- Show respect for the judge and obey his orders.

46

Trial by ordeal: A medical perspective

There's a prevailing opinion among physicians, which is strongly supported in many other quarters, that cases of malpractice are not tried in court on the basis of the medical facts and issues involved. All too often we hear of cases being won or lost by courtroom tricks, character assassination, and playing on the jury's emotions.

Such behavior isn't limited to the plaintiffs' bar; defendants' attorneys resort to it too. When the sums of money at stake are large and personal and professional reputations are on the line, restraint often flies out the window. Undoubtedly the adversary nature of our legal system is also responsible; lawyers like to win cases just as much as their clients do. Finally, "guilt" (liability) or "innocence" is seldom clear-cut in medical malpractice cases. Indeed, the basic question juries often have to decide is not "Was the doctor negligent?" but "Which expert can we believe?"

Malpractice does exist, and patients must have protection from thoughtless physicians. But emotional clouding of the issues, exercises in irrelevancy, and intellectual subversion are no way to assure it. The result is only increased antagonism between attorney and physician, with growing cynicism on the part of the laity. For the defendant, medical fact witness, or expert opinion witness, therefore, malpractice trials can truly be trials by ordeal.

The fact witness probably has the easiest time—as long as he's sure of his facts. If you're summoned as a fact witness and your testimony is airtight, you can be reasonably sure of leaving the courtroom with reputation and livelihood intact.

The expert witness has much more to lose. If you're testifying as an expert, you can expect the opposing attorney to do all he can to discredit your testimony. He may try to do it by attacking your personal integrity and professional reputation. You're required to maintain your objectivity while being accused of bias (after all, you're testifying for one of the two parties to the case), to educate a lay jury without condescension, to state your opinions forthrightly without appearing arrogant, to answer questions truthfully without knowing their intent, and to protect your reputation as an expert. Yet there are physicians who thrive on such challenges. And if you don't relish walking so many tightropes, you have the option, unless served with a subpoena, of refusing to offer your testimony.

It's the defendant for whom a malpractice trial can truly be a nightmare. Many physicians who have been sued for malpractice, even those who have won their cases, have suffered serious damage to their health, seen their marriages break up under the strain, and lost patients by droves. Rather than face the risk of another malpractice suit, some doctors retire from private practice.

"I was frustrated, angry, and hurt that this was happening to me," says an Illinois family physician who was sued—and won—twice. "I worried about the effect the publicity was having on my wife and children. The stress and tension were having a noticeably adverse effect on my health. For a time, I considered getting out of medicine altogether. I hated the thought of giving up a profession that I loved and had devoted my entire life to, but it just wasn't worth practicing anymore."

However blameless he may be, the physician who's sued for malpractice cannot be confident that his case will be decided on its medical merits. It's very difficult to dispel certain ideas that are firmly entrenched in the minds of the lay public who compose juries. One such idea, as mentioned in Chapter 2, is the equation of failure to cure cancer with failure to diagnose it "early enough." Not only is this fallacious, but it also contradicts current medical knowledge.[1-8]

Let's suppose you've been sued by the widower of a woman who died of extensive metastases originating in cancer of the breast. You had observed the highest standards of diagnosis and treatment with this patient, but, as often happens, her bereaved husband is sure that had you only "caught it in time" you could have cured her of cancer. The plaintiff's attorney has exploited that idea for all it's worth in his direct examination. Now it's your turn. Your lawyer calls several "expert witnesses." First to take the stand is Pietro M. Gullino, M.D., of the Laboratory of Pathophysiology, National Cancer Institute:[4]

> The question here is whether detection and removal of a primary breast carcinoma of 0.5 cm. as contrasted to 3 cm. in diameter has any real impact on the future evolution of the disease, and consequently, whether ef-

> forts should be made to detect the asymptomatic breast carcinoma.
>
> Our present knowledge of the mechanism of metastasis formation suggests that a primary breast carcinoma can metastasize when it is constituted by a relatively small number of cells that is far beyond our present capacity of detection. . . .
>
> Retrospective surveys have shown that breast carcinomas treated in Stage I of the TNM [tumor, node, metastasis] classification have much better prognoses than those treated in later stages.[4, 9] One must remember, however, that retrospective surveys have also shown that survival does not necessarily improve when the interval between tumor detection and removal is the shortest. The longest survival is often seen in those patients with a primary lesion that has been present for months but without any clinically evident metastases.[2, 10-12] These observations support the theory that the growth potential of a primary tumor and its metastases is a predetermined property of the cell population at its inception.[7] . . .
>
> Indeed, retrospective analyses of breast cancer case histories indicate that early diagnosis increases survival time only in a fraction of cases.[13] If early diagnosis is used synonymously with curability today, one must take into consideration that only a fraction of Stage I carcinomas is involved. The belief that early diagnosis and treatment can eliminate the primary tumor before metastasis occurs is unsubstantiated and goes against the evidence presented above.

Next to "testify" are Lauren V. Ackerman, M.D., Department of Pathology, Health Sciences Center, State University of New York, Stony Brook, and Anna Luise Katzenstein, M.D., Division of Surgical Pathology, Washington University School of Medicine, St. Louis:[1]

> Patients with small cancers as a group do better than patients with large cancers. But sophisticated studies made by LeGal and Igot[7] show that many cancers at the time of clinical discovery are already disseminated. Tubiana[14] noted that 50% of the breast cancers he studied had metastasized at least two years before the primary

tumor became clinically detectable (1 cm.). The growth rate of the primary cancer seemed to have little influence on the probability of metastatic dissemination by the tumor cell. In other words, so-called minimal breast cancer, unfortunately, may already be disseminated and therefore is not early but late.

Finally, your attorney calls R. S. Handley, M.D., Middlesex Hospital, London:[5]

> Much emphasis has been laid in programmes of public education on the point that the earlier a tumour is treated the more likely it is to be cured. This seems self-evident, but voices have been raised, most notably by Sutherland (1960), to suggest that the effect of early treatment may not always be as dramatic as is generally suggested.
>
> My own evidence . . . shows that the difference in the crude five-year survival figures is astonishingly small. . . . The 10-year survival . . . does begin to show the result which might be expected but it is not as marked as one might have hoped until one reaches the long-delay group. Even here the figure of 26% is surprising because it might have been supposed that all would be dead. . . . It here appears that delay has no effect on survival [at 15 years], but the number of patients in the various groups is perhaps too small for any very definite conclusion.
>
> If we analyse this same series of patients to see what effect delay has on clinical staging at the first consultation, we find almost the same lack of correlation between delay and stage . . . perhaps slightly more relationship between these two factors but not much. The same may be said of the effect of delay on histological findings in the axillary and internal mammary lymph nodes. . . .
>
> These results do not make me feel that we ought to relax our efforts to get patients to treatment as early as possible, but they do suggest that such facile optimism as the view that the mortality of breast cancer could be reduced to one-seventh of its present size by adequate treatment within a month of the onset of symptoms is not credible. The situation was ably, and in my view correctly, summed up by Kreyberg (1953) when he said: . . . "We must, however, always have in mind that the benefit is

statistically moderate, and we ought to be modest in our claims as to the possibility of materially altering the situation for the breast carcinoma patients by this approach to the problem" [i.e., early diagnosis].

The defense rests. There's no cross-examination in our hypothetical trial; the "experts" have made their arguments convincingly. But the jury has the last word.

References

1. Ackerman LV, Katzenstein AL: The concept of minimal breast cancer and the pathologist's role in the diagnosis of "early carcinoma." *Cancer* 39:2755, 1977
2. Brooke BN: Early detection of cancer. *Lancet* 2:1289, 1968
3. Fisher ER, Redmond C, Fisher B: A perspective concerning the relation of duration of symptoms to treatment failure in patients with breast cancer. *Cancer* 40:3160, 1977
4. Gullino PM: Natural history of breast cancer. *Cancer* 39:2697, 1977
5. Handley RS: Observations and thoughts on cancer of the breast. *Proc R Soc Med* 65:437, 1972
6. Kreyberg L: Significance of "early diagnosis" in breast cancer: Study of some common usages of term. *Br J Cancer* 7:157, 1953
7. LeGal Y, Igot JP: Age des adénopathies métastatiques dans le cancer mammaire. *Ann Anat Pathol* 16:9026, 1971
8. Sutherland R: *Cancer, the Significance of Delay*. London: Butterworths, 1960
9. Burn JI: "Early" breast cancer: The Hammersmith trial. An interim report. *Br J Surg* 61:762, 1974
10. Bond WH: The influence of various treatments on survival rates in cancer of the breast. In *The Treatment of Carcinoma of the Breast* (Jarret AS, ed), pp 24-39. Amsterdam: Excerpta Medica, 1968
11. Denoix P: Treatment of malignant breast tumors: Recent results. *Cancer Res* 31:3, 1970
12. Smith JA III, Gamez-Araujo JJ, Gallager HS, et al: Carcinoma of the breast: Analysis of total lymph node involvement versus level of metastasis. *Cancer* 39:527, 1977
13. Zelen M: A hypothesis for the natural time history of breast cancer. *Cancer Res* 28:207, 1968
14. Tubiana M, Chauvel P, Renaud A, et al: Growth rate and natural history of human breast cancers. *Bull Cancer* 62:341, 1975

Index

A

B

C

D

E

F

G

H

I

N

O

P

R

S

T

U

V

W

X

Z